Environmental economics
Vol. 1. Theories

D1694986

With co-operation of

J. Blokland
T. H. Botterweg
F. Hartog
A. J. Hendriks
G. F. A. de Jong
L. H. Klaassen
J. G. Lambooy
P. Nijkamp
S. W. F. van der Ploeg
P. H. J. J. Terhal

Environmental economics

Vol. 1. Theories

Edited by

P. Nijkamp
**Professor of Regional Economics,
Free University, Amsterdam**

Martinus Nijhoff Social Sciences Division
Leiden 1976

Translated by J. v.d. Dool-Phelps

ISBN 90.207.0644.6

Printed in Belgium.

Contents

Contributors

Dr. J. BLOKLAND, National Physical Planning Agency, The Hague

Mr. T. H. BOTTERWEG, Netherlands Economic Institute, Rotterdam

Professor F. HARTOG, State University, Groningen

Professor A. J. HENDRIKS, Netherlands Economic Institute and Erasmus University, Rotterdam

Dr. G. F. A. DE JONG, Federation of Netherlands Industry, The Hague

Professor L. H. KLAASSEN, Netherlands Economic Institute and Erasmus University, Rotterdam

Professor J. G. LAMBOOY, University of Amsterdam, Amsterdam

Professor P. NIJKAMP, Free University, Amsterdam

Mr. S. W. F. VAN DER PLOEG, Institute for Environmental Studies, Free University, Amsterdam

Mr. P. H. J. J. TERHAL, Erasmus University, Rotterdam

Preface

'The river Rhine, it is well known,
Doth wash your city of Cologne;
But tell me, Nymphs, what power divine
Shall henceforth wash the river Rhine?'

The above strophe, composed by Samuel Taylor Coleridge early last century, shows that interest in environmental problems (in this case, the self-cleansing property of water) is not just something new, but was also present in the past. The reader may wonder, after this poetic contribution which is still very relevant, if there is any need to compile a book which handles environmental problems in a much less prosaic, i.e. scientific, way.
It is my firm belief that present environmental problems, because of both s i z e and i n t e n s i t y, deserve our profound attention. This concern will have to be shown not only by those directly involved, viz. the 'man in the street', but also by the authorities as well as by scientists. In view also of the social relevance of the environmental question, science may not be impartial but must make a (modest) attempt to analyse, explain and solve the present environmental question systematically.
This book does not pretend to provide the final, all-embracing answers to all environmental issues. It does aim at analysing various aspects of the environmental problems from the point of view of economic theory. I am convinced that the current urgency of the environmental problem, particularly in the western developed countries, is such that economics will be increasingly and sometimes unwillingly confronted by it.
This book attempts to provide a representative picture of the scientific environmental investigation which (in particular in the Netherlands) is being carried out by various economists practically involved in environmental quality studies. The emphasis of the book is on economic theory and environmental quality analysis. The meaning of this reader is not to provide abstract theories on environmental problems, but to show the practical implications and difficulties in applying economic theory to real-world environmental problems.
The second book '(Environmental economics, Vol. 2. Methods)' which is published simultaneously in this series focuses on a set of operational techniques and empirical models in environmental quality analysis.
I hope that both books will lead to a considerable deepening of understanding and to an extension of knowledge with regard to the

current environmental question within a broader group of interested people. The systematic approach of both volumes is also eminently suitable for study by planners, decision-makers and students in kindred sciences.

The first chapter of this book on the theory of environmental economics, is written by Prof. P. Nijkamp. This introductory chapter focuses on recent contributions to economic-ecologic evaluations of natural environments. Particular attention is given to the question whether ecology can provide economics with a set of evaluation methods. Although the answer is not entirely positive, it appears that during recent years considerable progress has been made to integrate ecologic criteria into economic decision-making.

The second article, by S. W. F. van der Ploeg, describes the relations which can be established between biological and ecological phenomena on the one hand and economic phenomena on the other hand. The author discusses a number of possibilities for the valuation of the loss of functions of the environment, and he illustrates his views by means of a number of ecologic-economic models and techniques.

The third article is the work of T. H. Botterweg and Prof. L. H. Klaassen. They broach the problem of what procedure to adopt if a certain technological-economic project (for example, an enclosure of estuaries) involves the violation of an ecologically valuable area. By using a new concept, so-called shadow projects, it is possible to provide a more reliable basis for a cost-benefit analysis in project evaluations.

In the next chapter, Prof. J. G. Lambooy analyses the problems of physical planning from an environmental point of view. Both a spatial (re)allocation of activities and the creation of specific 'environmental enclaves' (Mishan), in general, are seen to be unable to stop environmental damage. This is particularly so, if the possibilities and limitations of physical planning are taken into account.

The problems of an integrated socio-economic regional policy, which takes environmental effects into account, are described by J. Blokland and Prof. A. J. Hendriks. Within the framework of labour market restrictions, these problems are illustrated by an issue of current importance, i.e., whether the establishment of new enterprises (in this case an iron and steel works) in a region exceeds the socio-economic and ecological capacity of this region.

The implications of the costs of a more stringent environmental policy, particularly from the point of view of private economics, are then pointed out by G. F. A. de Jong. He pays attention to the various effects of policy principles ('the polluter pays') and policy alternatives (levies, retributions etc.).

The question whether a different economic system offers more possibilities for a solution of the environmental question is dealt with by Prof. F. Hartog. Given a pair of realistic alternatives, viz. a collectivist and a capitalist system, it appears to be not possible to make a decisive choice on economic grounds. Another problem which reaches beyond our borders is that of international environmental pollution. P. H. J. J. Terhal, who considers this problem, has concentrated on pollution of the ocean and the Green Revolution. In his article, he emphasizes very strongly the economic-political character of international environmental pollution and the need for international co-operation.

The articles contributed here by a number of different authors lead us in the first place to conclude that economists are working hard, from a variety of viewpoints and on all fronts, on the environmental problem. Indeed, a great number of different topics is being studied. It becomes evident from the different articles that, at the moment, there is not a systematic, integrated environmental analysis on a uniform basis. The steps which have been taken during the last years, can at most be regarded as the first tentative footsteps towards a full-grown environmental analysis and an economically justifiable environmental policy. Both in the theoretical field (in particular in the welfare-theoretical field of distribution effects and of evaluation methods) and in the policy field (in particular with regard to the co-ordination of environmental measures) a great deal of work has yet to be done.
It is my hope that this book will stimulate many economists and kindred scientists to develop the outlines presented here into an integrated procedure for environmental analysis and into adequate means of environmental control. May this book be of service in the protection of the creation of which our Maker said, in the beginning, 'Behold, it is very good'.

Amsterdam 1976   Peter Nijkamp

Economic-Ecologie Evaluation of Natural Environments

P. Nijkamp

1. Introduction

During the last decade several attempts have been made by ecologists to evaluate natural environments, rural landscapes, forests and trees, and so forth. An evaluation of natural environments is increasingly required in order to weigh alternative uses of natural environments against each other, particularly because environmental problems are going to be a major concern in physical planning. For example, in view of the large scale urbanization in western countries an evaluation of functions of rural landscapes versus urban landscapes is a necessary condition for making right decisions in the field of physical planning.

A good example of a useful evaluation of different types of landscapes is provided by McHarg (1969), who suggests the use of natural landscapes as the basis for planning urban developments. In his opinion an integrated view of natural and urban landscapes in physical planning will guarantee a total high-quality environment for man.

The increased interest in environmental problems has confronted planners with a set of environmental concerns and new methods for dealing with them. A first condition for adequate planning decisions is the presence of information on ecological systems and on environmental impacts of human decisions. Unfortunately the information on which to base decisions concerning environmental impacts is frequently lacking or at least incomplete. The complexity of ecological systems and of environmental processes implies that environmental decision-making is sometimes necessarily based on a considerable amount of uncertainty, even if planners raise the right questions.

For the moment the most reasonable way is to take into account as many environmental effects as possible in physical and environmental planning, although one should be aware of the partially biased information on these effects. A systematic way for a reasonably comprehensive description, analysis and prediction of environmental effects is the use of ecological flow diagrams with a variety of circuits and transformations (cf. the material balance diagram) or of formal ecological models (cf. Antonini

1

et al. (1974) and Walters (1971)). A systematic way of dealing with
detailed ecological information systems is presented by Lyle and
Von Wodtke (1974).
A comprehensive way to analyse the effects of human activities upon
ecological and environmental variables is the use of a so-called
environmental impact matrix (cf. Edmunds and Letey
(1973)). Human activities are represented by the left vertical list
and their environmental consequences are included in the top horizontal list of the matrix. The elements of the matrix denote the
quantitative effects of the activities on the environmental characteristics. These elements may measure the quantitative effects between
activities and environmental factors in different ways depending on
the amount of information available. Even an ordinal ranking scale
running from 1 to 100 can be used to represent the relative order
of magnitude of certain environmental effects. A simple example
of such an environmental impact matrix is contained below, where
the effects of creating a new residential-industrial area on environmental characteristics are included.

Figure 1. 1. An environmental impact matrix

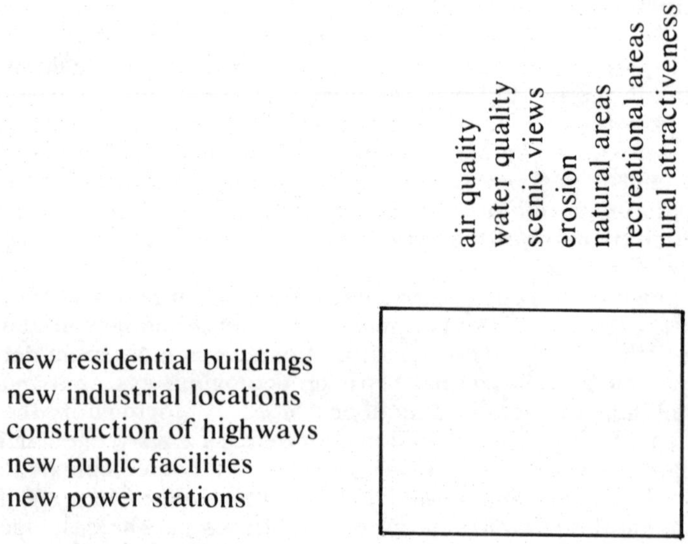

It is obvious that the use of impact matrices requires a lot of detailed information (cf. also the environmental models presented in
E. P. Odum (1971)). It should be noted that the causal links in an
environmental impact matrix may be more complex than indicated

above. For example, in addition to a d i r e c t effect of new industrial locations upon both air quality and natural areas, there may be an indirect second-order effect of air quality upon natural areas.

Given the environmental impacts of certain activities, the crucial question arises as to how to e v a l u a t e these effects, particularly if a choice has to be made among a set of alternatives. In this chapter a set of methods to evaluate environmental effects will be discussed, as they are recently developed in the ecological field. First, some methods to evaluate environmental factors in m o n e - t a r y units will be discussed, then attention will be paid to n o n - m o n e t a r y evaluation methods.

2. An assessment of the monetary value of wildlife

Commodities which have no easily measured market value (like trees, forests, animals, etc.) can only be evaluated by means of an indirect assessment. Some traditional methods in this field are a cost-benefit analysis and a cost-effectiveness analysis, but it is questionable whether these methods are reliable tools to assess intangible environmental effects and commodities. In the field of ecology some conceptual frameworks have been developed to assess the monetary values of wildlife.

An example of a monetary valuation of wildlife is contained in Ciriacy-Wantrup and Phillips (1970), who provided a monetary assessment of preserving the California tule elk. This monetary value (the 'social human benefits'), which was mainly based on the economic function of the elk population for hunters (via hunting permits, e.g.), was the result of a simple cost-benefit analysis.

In addition to the monetary aspects of preserving the elk population several other social and biological elements (like its value for natural sciences and for preserving a valuable gene-pool) were considered as well, but not transformed into monetary values. In spite of the limited scope of the study the authors exposed clearly the problems inherent to monetary valuations of wildlife.

Another attempt to assess the a m e n i t y v a l u e of wildlife was made by Helliwell (1967). In his analysis he considers a variety of factors which determine the attractiveness of woodlands and trees. By providing each factor with a certain score, depending on the quality of the factor at hand, then by aggregating all these scores and, finally, by multiplying the result with a monetary value, the monetary amenity value of trees and woodlands can be assessed. For example, the evaluation of woodlands depends on: a. area visible; b. position in landscape; c. average daylight viewing (urban) population; d. presence of other trees and woodlands; e. accessibility; f. species and state of crop; g. any special value. For a certain woodland its quality is represented as a score on a cardinal scale. The total score (aggregated in a multiplicative way) is then multiplied by a constant monetary factor (£ 10) to arrive at a final monetary amenity value of the woodlands concerned.

3

Helliwell calculates in a similar way the amenity values of trees. The valuation of trees rests on the following factors: a. crown area; b. useful life expectancy; c. importance of position in landscape or townscape; d. presence of other trees; e. form; f. species in relation to the setting; g. special or historical value. The monetary amenity value of a tree is again determined by aggregating the successive scores of a tree and by multiplying the result by a constant monetary term (£ 1/5).

It is evident that from an economic point of view a crucial problem is caused by the c o n s t a n t   m o n e t a r y   f a c t o r. It seems that this term is determined rather arbitrarily, so that the economic meaning of the previous operation is rather limited. The procedure does make sense for comparative purposes in assessing the relative values of woodlands or of trees, but even then a mutual comparison of woodlands or of trees can be carried out by considering only the aggregated (non-monetary) scores. The procedure does not have a meaning for evaluating d i f f e r e n t types of environmental commodities and does not touch upon the basic problem of a monetary valuation.

A second attempt to evaluate wildlife resources is contained in Helliwell (1969) by assessing the r e c o g n i z a b l e   b e n e f i t s of wildlife resources to man. These benefits can be subdivided into 7 categories: a. income from direct material and from returns from hunting, fishing etc. ; b. the maintenance of a reserve of genetic material for the breeding of new varieties of crop-producing plants and animals; c. the maintenance of natural populations of animals and plants as a buffer against unnaturally large increases in pest species; d. the education of children and adults; e. facilities for research and training of biologists; f. the natural history interest as the basis of a hobby for amateur naturalists, photographers etc. ; g. the local character at a certain place.

The benefits of factor a. can in principle be assessed directly on the basis of income from sold products and from the letting of shooting, fishing etc. The remaining factors, however, can only be evaluated in an indirect manner. The values of these factors are co-determined by their s c a r c i t y,   d i v e r s i t y,   and a c - c e s s i b i l i t y. For these 3 elements a scarcity index, a diversity index and an accessibility index can be created, respectively. Next, the order of magnitude of factors b. -g. can be determined as the (multiplicative) weighted average of the scarcity index, the diversity index and the accessibility index, where the weights are formed by the corresponding relevant size of the factor concerned in the wildlife resources (for example, area of land, number of species etc.). For example, the score for the factor 'education value' is calculated as: local scarcity index × number of obvious species × durability index × accessibility index. Next, the figure calculated so far for each factor separately is multiplied by a constant amount of money for each successive factor. Aggregation of the monetary amounts of all these separate factors gives the final monetary value of the wildlife resources concerned.

4

Apart from the weighting problem and the problem of precisely defining the factors, a crucial question is again: how to determine the monetary values of each factor separately? Helliwell suggests the indirect calculation of these multiplicative constant monetary units. For example, the value of natural areas for education and research may be associated with the cost of building and equipping additional laboratory facilities at schools and colleges.

It is clear that the aforementioned monetary values do not necessarily reflect the market values of the successive factors concerned. These imputed prices, however, seem to have a certain meaning in comparing alternative development plans for wildlife resources. In spite of a certain arbitrariness in determining these imputed values such a method may have some use in evaluating small-scale environmental goods in land-use planning, as was exemplified by Helliwell for a problem of evaluating the removal of hedgerows. Even then these methods are based on rather heroic assumptions concerning the monetary values for each factor (see for a critical comment Hooper (1970)).

A third proposal to evaluate wildlife was made by Helliwell (1971a) in relation to attractiveness of and visits to natural areas. In the United Kingdom the average expenditures on leisure, entertainment and recreation are approximately £ 5, 000 million. By means of a questionnaire among nature conservationists, town planners and landscape architects it was found that approximately 6% of these annual luxurious expenditures were made for visits to wildlife resources and natural areas. Given its total area, the capitalized value of wildlife would average about £ 300 per acre, an amount which corresponds approximately to the current market price for agricultural land.

The latter method bears a certain resemblance to evaluation methods of recreational areas based on demand curves for and expenditures to recreational items. However, this method, which is also frequently used in cost-benefit studies, is here used in a very crude manner. For example, it is questionable whether the implicit value of natural areas can be assessed by considering only luxurious expenditures. This problem of evaluating recreational areas is a heavy task in recreational studies. For the moment, the conclusion is that monetary evaluation methods based on an ecological assessment of wildlife seem to be not very successful. The second method developed by Helliwell, which is based on an assessment of the various functions of natural areas, appeared to be relatively more satisfactory than the other methods. A variant of such a functional evaluation method will now be discussed in more detail, based on an ecological study by Gosselink, E. P. Odum and Pope (1973).

The study carried out by Gosselink et al. concentrates primarily on the value of tidal marshes, but it has a more general scope. Wildlife resources like tidal marshes have a variety of functions (for example, nursery ground for fish and shellfish). The value of marshland stems from identifiable commercial and recreational functions for which monetary values can in principle be determined.

In addition to these direct functions marshland has a set of potential functions which might also be evaluated.

A first function of tidal marshes is related to commercial fishery. Therefore, one can assess the present value of a unit of marsh and its associated tidal creeks on the basis of the dependent fishery. By estimating the annual revenues of direct and indirect fishery for the tidal marshland concerned, the average capitalized value per acre of marshland can be calculated.

A second function of marshland is related to recreation (sport fishing, hunting, boating etc.). By aggregating the total amount of money spent on recreational purposes at the tidal marsh the recreational value per acre of marshland can be determined. By summing up the fishery revenue and the recreational revenue per acre of marshland the total average monetary value of an acre of marshland can be calculated.

In addition to these direct functions tidal marshes have a set of potential functions, which have not been completely realized so far in the natural area, but which could be realized in the future without affecting its more or less self-maintaining natural state (for instance, intensive aquaculture, but no industrial use). A first potential use may be oyster aquaculture, which requires only a minor modification of the estuary. The expected annual revenues of oyster aquaculture can in principle be estimated, so that the potential value of an acre of marshland can be assessed for this additional function.

The same holds true for the waste treatment that active ecosystems can accomplish without appreciable reduction in water quality. The waste assimilated by an estuary can be measured in terms of BOD (biochemical oxygen demand) load. Assuming that an estuary is capable of providing a rather extensive waste treatment, one can calculate the value of the estuary on the basis of the average treatment costs of water-purifying installations. It is obvious that this value is only valid in as far as the waste-loading capacity of estuaries is not exceeded. Otherwise, one has to estimate the additional costs to increase the water quality up to a desired level. It appears that in general the value of marshland with respect to waste treatment is rather important.

Other marsh functions (like its role in global cycles of nitrogen and sulfur, the possible buffer function against storms, and the protection of beautiful white sand beaches) can in principle be evaluated in the same way, although certain other functions (like the habitat function for migratory birds such as the snow goose and the blue goose) are very hard to evaluate.

By aggregating the monetary values of the foregoing marsh functions, the total maximum value per acre of marshland can be estimated. This final result is indeed a maximum value in as far as certain actual and potential functions are conflicting. On the other hand, this final value may be an underestimation in as far as certain items could not be quantified in monetary terms.

Therefore, one may question whether such a functional component approach should not be replaced by a more integral approach to a life-support system. Furthermore, one may question whether indeed the f u n c t i o n s of the ecosystem concerned are evaluated, or whether only the o u t p u t (in terms of fishery and recreation) is evaluated. There seems to be a significant discrepancy between the e c o l o g i c a l functions of the ecosystem in question and its u s e f o r m a n. An alternative, integral approach will be discussed in the next section.

3. P r o d u c t i v e e n e r g y f l o w s a s a b a s i s f o r m o n e - t a r y v a l u a t i o n s

Recently, several ecologists have stated that an ecological system can be evaluated in e n e r g y terms. In this approach energy flow modelling is used as the integrating mechanism for describing the processes in an ecosystem. This approach is based on the fact that all ecosystems carry on energy transfer processes, so that energy flows can be used as a common denominator to unite interactions of all kinds.

These energetic value theories were mainly proposed by H. T. Odum (1971), and further developed for land use planning by Antonini et al. (1974) and by E. P. Odum and H. T. Odum (1972). The essential assumption in these energetic value theories is that natural areas are a necessary part of man's total environment. The e x c h a n g e of e n e r g y a n d m o n e y is essentially the basis for economic transactions, so that the ratio of Gross National Product to National Energy Consumption can be used to equate energy with money. It appears that in the United States approximately 10^{16} kilocalories are required yearly to produce a Gross National Product of 10^{12} dollars, so that one dollar corresponds approximately to 10^4 kilocalories. An application of this energetic value theory was present-ed by Gosselink et al. (1973) in their study about the value of the tidal marsh.

The amount of primary production in a life-support system is a certain measure of the energy flow of a natural community, and hence an indicator for the useful work that might in principle be accomplished. This amount of energy can then be used to evaluate. in monetary units any part of a natural area where primary pro-duction can be measured or estimated. Consequently, the income-capitalization value of an acre of marshland can be approximated in a straightforward way. The latter approach assesses the integral value of a delimited natural area without specifying the various functions or uses, so that the problem of conflicting uses can be overcome in this way. It appears that in general the energetic valuation procedure leads to considerably higher monetary values for natural areas than the functional component approach.

The value of marshland determined in the aforementioned way may play a significant role in land-use design. If the relatively high energetic prices for natural areas are accepted by physical planners and local agencies, valuable marshlands will less easily be destroyed or transformed into competitive uses (like industrial areas). In as far as marshlands are privately owned, one can now in principle assess the compensating amount of money to be paid to the owner in order to prevent him from transforming the marshlands into more profitable states (like the use as an industrial area). In addition, one should take into consideration that frequently an alternative use of marshlands implies an irreversible action (at least in the short run). Here a traditional demand analysis in which the price of a commodity is determined by its relative availability cannot be applied in a satisfactory way, since there is hardly any possibility to shift a certain realized development back to the original state of the tidal marsh.

The aforementioned approach is obviously of a more general nature. It is also relevant for the valuation of forests, rural areas and so forth. A reasonable solution to the problem of development alternatives is to specify a p r i o r i a land-use plan which delimits the amount and location of natural areas on the basis of information about a desirable future level of urban-industrial development. Then such areas might be zoned into the public domain, before the process of land speculation raises the market price. The latter approach, however, requires a reasonable compartmentalization between developed and undeveloped areas. By making use of the energetic value theory in principle a reasonable compartmentalization can be obtained (see E. P. Odum and H. T. Odum (1972)).

The foregoing energetic valuation procedure will now be illustrated by means of an example from the Netherlands. In the Northeastern part of the Netherlands recently several plans have been developed for improving the hydrological conditions of some agricultural hinterland areas. A first development plan would require the construction of a new canal through a valuable estuary, called the Dollard. The implementation of this plan would destroy approximately 600 hectares of this estuary.

Now the problem arises: how to evaluate the value of this area? One of the possibilities to gauge the monetary value of the area in question is to use the primary energy production of this ecosystem. On the basis of ecological information derived from Gosselink et al. (1973) the average primary energy production of an estuary appears to be approximately 10^8 kcal per hectare.

Gross national energy consumption in the Netherlands during the year 1974 was approximately 705×10^{12} kcal. The value of national product (against market prices) during the same period was approximately 170×10^9 Dfl. Hence the conversion ratio between production and energy is equal to $1 : 4.1 \times 10^3$.

Given the latter conversion ratio the annual value of 1 hectare of the estuary is approximately equal to $10^8/(4.1 \times 10^3) = 24.4 \times 10^3$ Dfl. Therefore, the total energy value of 600 hectares of the estuary is approximately 146×10^5 Dfl. for the year 1974.

If a discount rate of 9 per cent is assumed and if the terminal period is assumed to correspond with the year 2000, the total capitalized value of the area concerned is approximately 16×10^7 Dfl. The construction of this new canal through the estuary had to be evaluated against a more expensive plan, where the canal had to be digged around this area. In spite of the fact that this plan would cost several millions of Dutch guilders extra, the government has taken the decision to implement the latter plan in order to preserve the natural area formed by the estuary. A more extensive discussion of all costs and benefits of this alternative plan can be found in Nijkamp and Verhage (1975).

The energetic valuation procedure appears to provide a rather operational method to assess the value of natural areas, plants, trees, etc. The basic assumption is that man lives by material and energy, so that the extent to which a man-made system is compatible with the natural environment can only be judged in terms of these variables. Therefore, the material and energy flow characteristics of an ecological system are of primary concern (cf. Koenig, Edens and Cooper (1975)).

A basic problem in applying these energetic valuation methods is the fact that the natural environment may have several other functions in addition to material and energy deliveries. For example, it may be a source of spiritual well-being, of knowledge or of inspiration. Even an area with a low energetic value may have a high implicit value due to beautiful scenic views, so that in addition to the energy contents its quality seems to be important. This implies that an energetic valuation method cannot be considered as a general method to evaluate intangible effects in market prices. Its relevance is limited to natural areas and natural goods which have a clear energetic function. Furthermore, this energetic valuation procedure takes for granted the rightness of actual national or regional income, so that this method includes all shortcomings in the use of national or regional income as a measure for the value of national or regional welfare (the latter problem will not be dealt with here). Hence, inaccuracies are implicit in this method.

The advantage of the energy approach is the comprehensive way of evaluating natural areas and natural goods by coping with the important problem of mutually non-exclusive and interdependent functions of natural areas and goods.

Having considered the various ways to evaluate ecological goods in monetary terms, we will now turn to alternative methods to evaluate these goods in quantitative terms without using monetary units as a measuring rod.

4. A functional valuation of environmental goods

An alternative way of estimating the relative importance of environmental goods (natural areas, parks, animals, etc.), is to analyse the various functions of these goods for man (cf. Bouma (1972) and Helliwell (1971a)). Environmental goods provide a multiplicity of indispensable or desirable functions like a source of raw materials, of energy and food, a stabilizer in natural and man-made systems, a signal function for external perturbations, a source for human health, a recreational and aesthetic function, a scientific, educational and artistic function, or an ethical function per se.

The foregoing functions can in principle be approximated for almost each function separately. For example, the productive value of a forest may be assessed by means of its total production in terms of wood, rubber, etc.; the scientific value of a forest may be approximated as the sum total of all research funds oriented to the forest in question, etc.

For a unit of natural area the various functions can be represented as a vector f (a so-called f u n c t i o n a l   e n v i r o n m e n t a l p r o f i l e); each element f_i (i = 1, ..., I) of f indicates the quantitative value of the area for the corresponding function. It should be noted that such a numerical representation of environmental functions is based on a set of multidimensional characteristics. The dimensions might be translated into comparable units by representing the numerical outcomes of the functions on a cardinal ranking scale running from 1 to 100. If several units of natural areas are to be considered, a similar result can be achieved by means of a statistical standardization for each function over all areas, so that the transformed outcomes f_i^* are equal to:

$$f_i^* = \frac{f_i - \bar{f}}{s} \tag{4.1}$$

where $\bar{f}$ is the mean of the variable concerned and s its standard deviation.

By aggregating the scores f_i^* of all functions a total value v of the area concerned is obtained, i.e.,

$$v = \sum_{i=1}^{I} f_i^* \tag{4.2}$$

The foregoing numerical valuation of the area in question may also result from a w e i g h t e d aggregation of all separate functional scores, provided that ecologists can supply sufficient information concerning the relative importance of all functions in the total ecosystem. Obviously, the latter approach would require an interplay between economists and ecologists in order to indicate precisely the basis for such a weighting procedure (for example, societal interests, ecological requirements etc.).

The environmental valuation of a certain area does make sense for mutual comparisons of natural areas where all functions are defined consistently. In this way a functional environmental profile can be used in physical planning and landscape planning as a tool for relative evaluations.

A basic problem is that many functions may have a considerable

10

area of overlap, or that some functions may be conflicting (see also Section 2). Its advantage is that a monetary valuation procedure is not necessary to assess the environmental value of natural areas or parks. It should be noted here that a monetary economic evaluation method like a cost-benefit analysis is essentially an evaluation method which attempts to transform the numerical values of all functions into monetary measuring units, but the previous procedure indicates that such a monetary transformation is not always necessary. The basic problem in applying these functional environmental profiles is: how to use such environmental profiles in a broader framework of environmental analysis and environmental decision-making? The latter problem is essentially the subject matter of multi-criteria analysis and multi-criteria decision-making (see Nijkamp (1975)).

5. Ecological qualities as a basis for environmental valuations

As set out in the previous paragraph, ecological or natural functions may provide an operational functional valuation method for environmental goods, but the sometimes conflicting and non-exhaustive nature of this valuation procedure obviates its applicability. This is the reason why recently ecologists have focused their attention on ecological quality characteristics as a basis for environmental valuations (cf. Duffey (1971), Helliwell (1971a, b, 1973, 1974), Hooper (1971), McHarg (1969), E. P. Odum (1971), Regier and Cowell (1972), Van der Maarel (1971), Van der Ploeg (1972), Stearns and Montag (1974) and Tubbs and Blackwood (1971)). Instead of a set of functions, here natural areas, parks, trees and so forth are characterised by a set of ecological quality indicators. [1] These quality indicators are inter alia: diversity of species and of the ecosystem in question, rarity of species and of communities, and so forth.
Most of these ecological quality indicators can in principle be quantified and next included in a vector q. For example, the diversity of a community can be conceived of as a ratio of the number of species (N) with respect to the number of individuals per species (I). According to E. P. Odum (1971) the diversity d can be calculated as:

$$d = \frac{N}{\log I} \qquad (5.1)$$

In this way all elements of q can be approximated. The elements q_j $(j = 1, \ldots, J)$ of q constitute an environmental quality profile, and can be used to characterise environmental goods in an operational way.
The same scoring procedure as set out in the previous section can be used to obtain a total numerical value for the environmental

goods concerned. If the transformed score is denoted by q_j^* (j = 1, ..., J), the total value v of the environmental good concerned is:

$$v = \sum_{j=1}^{J} q_j^* \qquad (5.2)$$

where the assumption is made that, within a certain range, a higher value of q_j^* represents a more desirable state of the ecosystem concerned. This indicator can also be calculated as a weighted average of all q_j^*'s over a set of areas. The latter method can be used in a similar way for comparison purposes in land use planning and ecosystem planning. Its usefulness may still be increased by constructing a certain average standard norm for ecological quality of certain areas. In this case the relative deviation with respect to the standard norm can be calculated as well. Such an analysis can also be used as a critical path analysis in order to detect when an ecological perturbation will affect plants, animals and man.
The foregoing method concentrates in particular on the state (or actual quality) of environmental goods. Interactions between elements of an environmental profile are left out of consideration. An analysis of these interactions would require the use of ecological flow diagrams or dynamic ecological models. The dynamics of the quality of environmental goods may be studied by means of a comparative static analysis of the environmental profiles from successive periods.
The foregoing environmental quality profiles may be used to analyse in more detail the structure of environmental goods by making a distinction between several components like landscape, botanical situation and ornithological situation. In this case the environmental quality vector q is extended to an e n v i r o n m e n t a l q u a l i t y m a t r i x Q.
An application of the latter method is contained in an ecological valuation study of the South-Western part of the Netherlands (see Werkgroep Zuidwest-Nederland (1972)). By means of scoring methods for each region a total ecological value could be approximated. Alternative applications are found in Livingston (1975), and Malcolm and MacDonald (1975).
A slightly different approach was adopted by McHarg (1969), who made also a distinction between various ecological quality factors like wildlife, hydrological situation, climatological conditions and so forth. Each of these factors was again provided with a score indicating the state of the factor concerned.
Next, a series of possible functional g o a l s of the environmental area concerned was specified (like conservation, recreation, residential use, industrial use, etc.). For each separate goal the relative importance of each factor in attaining the goal in question can in principle be indicated on a ranking scale.
The foregoing goal attainment procedure is represented in matrix form in Figure 5.2.

12

Figure 5.1. An environmental quality profile matrix

environmental quality indicators	landscape · botanical situation · ornithological situation
1 . . . . J	Q

Figure 5.2. An environmental quality matrix for various uses of natural areas

environmental quality factors	conservation · recreation · residential use · industrial use
1 . . . . J	

The latter matrix may be useful for calculating the relative importance of a certain area in realizing one of the targets of land use. It also can be used directly for a comparison of different areas. It is evident, that the foregoing ecological quality analyses require a lot of detailed information which is not always sufficiently available. Hence these analyses suffer sometimes from a certain degree of uncertainty.

6. Conclusion

The foregoing ecological valuation methods show that monetary evaluations of environmental goods have to cope with many problems. A unique market price is in general not available, so that indirect assessment procedures have to be applied. Even then a monetary valuation is frequently not very successful. For the moment the functional approach based on direct and potential uses as well as the energetic approach appear to be rather successful, albeit that a number of refinements have to be carried out before these approaches can be used in land use and environmental planning. The non-monetary valuation methods (particularly the environmental quality profiles) open in principle more possibilities of deriving values of environmental goods.
A basic problem of the latter class of valuation methods is: how to use these methods in a planning and policy framework where a variety of other economic effects has to be taken into account? In this case the profile methods are only meaningful, if the other economic effects can also be evaluated in non-monetary terms.
This brings us back again to the problem of multi-criteria decision-making. This topic is discussed in more detail in Nijkamp (1975).

Note

1. This idea is closely related to the so-called 'social indicators movement' (see Smith (1973)).

References

Antonini, G. A. , K. C. Ewel, and J. J. Ewel, 'Ecological Modelling of a Tropical Watershed: A Guide to Regional Planning', Spatial Aspects of Development (B. S. Hoyle, ed.), Wiley, New York, 1974, pp. 52-74.
Bouma, F. , 'Evaluatie van Natuurfuncties', Institute for Environmental Studies, Free University, Amsterdam, 1972 (mimeographed).
Bouma, F. , and S. W. F. van der Ploeg, 'Functies van de Natuur; een Economisch-Ecologische Analyse', Institute for Environmental Studies, Amsterdam, 1975 (mimeographed).

Ciriacy-Wantrup, S. V. , and W. E. Phillips, 'Conservation of the California Tule Elk: A Socio-economic Study of a Survival Problem', Biological Conservation, vol. 3, no. 1, 1970, pp. 23-32.

Duffey, E. , 'The Management of Woolwalton Fen: A Multidisciplinary Approach', The Scientific Management of Animal and Plant Communities for Conservation (E. Duffey and A. S. Watt, eds.), Blackwell Scientific Publishing Comp. , Oxford, 1971, pp. 581-597.

Edmunds, S. , and J. Letey, Environmental Administration. McGraw-Hill, New York, 1973.

Gosselink, J. G. , E. P. Odum, and R. M. Pope, 'The Value of the Tidal Marsh', Marine Science Department, Louisiana State University, Baton Rouge, 1973 (mimeographed).

Helliwell, D. R. , 'The Amenity Value of Trees and Woodlands', The Arboricultural Association Journal, vol. 1, no. 5, 1967, pp. 128-131.

Helliwell, D. R. , 'Valuation of Wildlife Resources', Regional Studies, vol. 3, no. 1, 1969, pp. 41-47.

Helliwell, D. R. , 'A Methodology for the Assessment of Priorities and Values in Nature Conservation', Merlewood Research and Development Paper, no. 28, 1971a (mimeographed).

Helliwell, D. R. , 'Changes in Flora and Fauna Associated with the Afforestation of a Scottish Moor - An Evaluation', Merlewood Research and Development Paper, no. 29, 1971b (mimeographed).

Helliwell, D. R. , 'An Examination of the Effects of Size and Isolation on the Wildlife Conservation Value of Wooded Sites', Merlewood Research and Development Paper, no. 49, 1973 (mimeographed).

Helliwell, D.R. , 'The Value of Vegetation for Conservation', Journal of Environmental Management, vol. 2, no. 1, 1974, pp. 51-78.

Hooper, M. D. , 'Critique of D. R. Helliwell: Valuation of Wildlife Resources', Regional Studies, vol. 4, no. 2, 1970, pp. 127-128.

Hooper, M. D. , 'The Size and Surroundings of Nature Reserves', The Scientific Management of Animal and Plant Communities for Conservation (E. Duffey and A. S. Watt, eds.), Blackwell Scientific Publishing Co. , Oxford, 1971, pp. 555-561.

Koenig, H. E. , T. C. Edens, and W. E. Cooper, 'Ecology, Engineering and Economics', Proceedings of the IEEE, vol. 63, no. 3, 1975, pp. 501-511.

Livingston, R. C. , 'Comprehensive Indicator: Quality of Life', Regional Environmental Management (L. E. Coate and P. A. Bonner, eds.), Wiley, New York, 1975, pp. 155-172.

Lyle, J. , and M. von Wodtke, 'An Information System for Environmental Planning', Journal of the American Institute of Planners, vol. 40, 1974, pp. 394-413.

Malcolm, D. G. , and D. MacDonald, 'Environmental Indicators for San Diego', Regional Environmental Management (L. E. Coate and P. A. Bonner, eds.), Wiley, New York, 1975, pp. 121-137.

Manners, I. R. , and M. W. Mikesell (eds.), Perspectives on Environment. Association of American Geographers (Commission on College Geography), Washington, 1974.

McHarg, I. L. , Design with Nature. Natural History Press, New York, 1969.

Nijkamp, P. , 'A Multi-Criteria Analysis for Project Evaluation', Papers of the Regional Science Association, vol. 35, 1975, pp. 87-111.

Nijkamp, P. , and C. Verhage, 'Cost-Benefit Analysis and Optimal Control Theory for Environmental Decisions: A Case Study of the Dollard Estuary', Paper at the Conference on Regional Science, Energy and Environment, Louvain, 1975.

Odum, E. P. , Fundamentals of Ecology. Saunders, Philadelphia, 1971.

Odum, E. P. , and H. T. Odum, 'Natural Areas as Necessary Components of Man's Total Environment', Transactions of the North American Wildlife and National Resources Conference, vol. 37, 1972, pp. 178-189.

Odum, H. T. , Environment, Power and Society. Wiley, New York, 1971.

Regier, H. A. , and E. B. Cowell, 'Applications of Ecosystem Theory; Succession, Diversity Stability, Stress and Conservation', Biological Conservation, vol. 4, no. 2, 1972, pp. 83-88.

Smith, D. M. , The Geography of Social Well-Being. McGraw-Hill, New York, 1973.

Stearns, F. , and T. Montag, The Urban Ecosystem. Dowden, Hutchinson & Ross, Stroudsburg (Pennsylvania), 1974.

Tubbs, C. R. , and J. W. Blackwood, 'Ecological Evaluation of Land for Planning Purposes', Biological Conservation, vol. 3, no. 3, 1971, pp. 169-172.

Van der Maarel, E. , 'Florastatistieken als Bijdrage tot de Evaluatie van Natuurgebieden', Gorteria, vol. 5, 1971, pp. 176-188.

Van der Ploeg, S. W. F. , 'Oecologie en Economie', Institute for Environmental Studies, Free University, Amsterdam, 1972 (mimeographed).

Walters, C. J. , 'Systems Ecology: The Systems Approach and Mathematical Models in Ecology', Fundamentals of Ecology (E. P. Odum, ed.), Saunders, Philadelphia, 1971, pp. 276-292.

Werkgroep Zuidwest-Nederland, De Kleuren van Zuidwest-Nederland - Visie op Milieu en Ruimte. Kontaktkommissie Nationale Landschapsbescherming, Amsterdam, 1972.

Ecology and Economics: Synthesis or Antithesis?

S. W. F. van de Ploeg

1. Introduction

In recent years, expressions such as 'ecological economics' or 'ecological approach of economics' have appeared with increased frequency in publications concerned with environmental problems. It is, however, not always clear what is actually meant by this coupling of concepts. Must economics be based on ecological laws? Is economic activity influenced by ecological processes?
These questions seem to be significant, since economics, as a science with an explanatory and predicting function with regard to economic activity should somehow take into account non-economic structures and processes which can affect that economic activity, in order to achieve the best possible approximation of reality. This becomes all the more cogent since economic lines of thought are often pursued in preference to others (cf. Bouma and Van der Ploeg, 1975).
It is possible to conceive a relation between 'economics' and 'non-economics' at different levels. Which are the subjects and which are the objects? What is the position of the economic science towards other sciences? What is the relationship between economic and non-economic models? How do economic and non-economic views affect political decisions?
In this chapter, the relationship between economics and one of the non-economic environmental sciences, ecology, will be described more fully.
A few introductory remarks on ecology follow in Section 2. In Section 3 the relationship between ecology and economics will be examined from both a methodological and political point of view. On the strength of these relationships, some 'ecological-economic' models will be considered in Section 4. Finally, in Section 5, governmental policy will again be considered, in the light of our conclusions.
As an ecologist, the present author does not pretend to put forward new economic ideas. This article aims only at contributing to the discussion on the possibilities - and difficulties - of economics.

2. What is ecology?

Nowadays, ecology is often wrongly regarded as a kind of belief:
a 'be kind to the environment' attitude. Sometimes it represents
a kind of panacea of sciences - an omni-science. The predicted
'ecological crisis' has much in common with a fashionable portrayal
of the Day of Judgement.
The reality is, as usual, rather less fanciful. Ecology is still a
science and not an ideology or policy instrument. It is a science
concerned with the study of organisms in, and in relation to, their respective surroundings (surroundings
means 'environment' here, i. e. the aggregate of external factors
with which an organism maintains relations). Besides this accent
on inter-relationships, two other characteristics of ecology are
stressed in this interpretation. Firstly, ecology concerns living
beings in their world; ecology of a stone or a glass of water is
therefore impossible. Secondly, man is not explicitly mentioned.
He is seen as one of the components of the biosphere (i. e. that part
of the earth where life exists).
On both historical (see, for example, Nelissen, 1972, p. 18) and
practical grounds, ecology can be subdivided into human ecology
and bio-ecology. This division is justifiable on scientific grounds
alone, since it is questionable whether human sciences and non-
human sciences are on the same level and whether the nature of their
subject-object relation is comparable (see Van der Ploeg, 1972,
p. 4). Moreover, although man is part of nature, the position he
occupies is a very special one. (2)
A further sub-division is of course possible. Human ecology can be
divided into biotic-human and social-human ecology. (3) For bio-
ecology, a distinction between plants and animals would seem to be
less relevant than a classification according to trophic ('food')
levels (E. P. Odum, 1971, pp. 8-11).

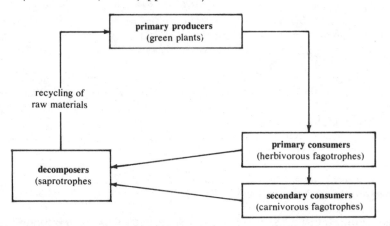

The sub-division of human ecology into individual and social aspects
can be compared with the classical division into autecology and

s y n e c o l o g y. The following diagram can then be drawn.

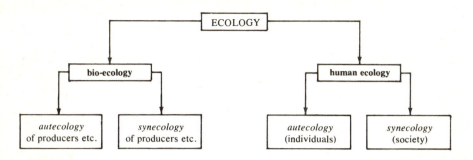

The biosphere can be called a system ('system' being here an
organized whole of inter-related components) (Keuning, 1973, p. 67).
Within this system, a set of sub-systems can be distinguished which
are to a certain extent independent of each other: the so-called
e c o s y s t e m s. A bio-ecosystem includes all (groups of) organisms
in relation to each other and to the abiotic (non-living) environment
(E. P. Odum, 1971, p. 5), while a human ecosystem represents a
community of people in relation to each other and to their environment. There is no general agreement on this topic; Nelissen (1972)
regards man as a part of more or less natural bio-ecosystems,
while Bos (1972, p. 263) sees man as an i n i t i a t o r in the cultural
or human ecosystems. It certainly does not seem wrong to assume
that in some cases (especially in primitive cultures, see for example H. T. Odum, 1971, p. 104), man, possibly in a cultural sub-
ecosystem, belongs to a bio-ecosystem. (4) In any case, human
society occupies a very special position in the biosphere system.
Moreover, because man's relationship with his environment (the
non-human part in particular) is to a certain extent 'biological',
biotic human ecology can in a way be seen as a link between bio-
ecology and social-human ecology. Actually, if this is so, it would
probably be better to describe ecology as the science which studies
the s t r u c t u r e a n d f u n c t i o n o f e c o s y s t e m s (cf. Kessler,
1973, thesis II).
Our tentative conclusion here is that although the definitions of
'ecology' are directive, they offer few opportunities for a scientific approach in which all organisms are sufficiently involved. In
the following sections, we will show that this conclusion impedes
an analysis of the relationships between ecology and economics.

3. The relationships between ecology and eco-
n o m i c s

When looking for a relationship between sciences (or between the
fields of sciences), the first question to arise is whether it is
possible to achieve a synthesis between those disciplines in order

to provide a more integrated picture of reality. If this synthesis is not possible, the question then arises to what extent these sciences conflict with each other with regard to certain aspects of reality. In other words, does parallel thinking in both sciences result in an antithesis with regard to reality? In this section, this matter will be considered in more detail. It is however very difficult to obtain an objective comparison of the various sciences because the language they use, arising from a specific vision of reality, is not uniform.

3.1. Philosophical aspects of the scientific method

If there is to be any relationship between economics and ecology, the philosophical aspects of the methods of both sciences must not differ too much. The relations induction/deduction and empiricism/rationalism are particularly important here. Because of the great heterogeneity of the subject matter of economics and ecology, an unambiguous characterization in a philosophical sense is not possible for either of them. In ecology, as well as in economics, deduction and induction go hand in hand (for example, a deduction based on a premise obtained by induction; see also Klant, 1972). Inductive thinking, however, dominates in autecology and deductive thinking in synecology (in both bio-ecology and human ecology). In economics, such a distinction is less pronounced: it is more concerned with the intellectual climate producing the theory.
The relationship between rationalistic and empirical influences seems to be of more importance. Bio-ecology and biotic-human ecology are in general of a distinctly empirical nature because they often concern 'biological' (or 'natural scientific') structures and processes. Social-human ecology (in so far as it is not of a phenomenological character) and economics sometimes tend towards a rationalistic approach, although in economics it would seem, rather, to be a difference between a 'normative' and a 'positive' approach.
Since World War II, the tendency to treat the social sciences (including economics) in a more empirical way has become stronger. It is not impossible that in the future an increasing number of theories and models in the social sciences will be constructed in an empirically-scientific way. This will, undoubtedly, result in an improvement in comparability. (5) The ceteris paribus clause (see Klant, 1972, pp. 116-119 for a detailed account) in economic theories, among others, is acceptable in bio-ecology, only if it is possible to test variations of factors which are assumed to be constant.

3.2. The philosophical structure of science

The subject-matter of a science describes the principles and limitations of that science. The comparison of their subject-matters can clarify the relationships between sciences.

The subject-matter of bio-ecology and human ecology has already been described in Section 2; that of economics can be described as the 'relationships between relatively scarce, alternatively usable goods and the totality of needs and ends served by those goods' (after Hennipman, 1962, p. 48).

Economics (with headings such as: scarcity of goods, need and choice) overlaps, therefore, a small part of the field covered by ecology (with headings such as: organisms, relationships and environment), i.e. that part where, for h u m a n b e i n g s in relation to their environment some choice is possible in the interaction between supply of and need for goods. (It is assumed in this view that a possible economics for animals and plants is not relevant.)

A f r a m e o f r e f e r e n c e of a science determines which themes are scientifically important and should cover in full all analyses of the empirical system concerned. (6)

Differences between subject-matters cause differences between frames of reference. The following descriptions of possible themes illustrate this:

a. For bio-ecosystems: energy circuits, nutrient cycles, food chains (and webs), diversity patterns in time and space, development and evolution, and control (cybernetics) (E. P. Odum, 1971).
b. For the 'community' in social ecology: the status quo and the dynamics of structural elements, of their relationships, their locations, the territorial and temporal organizations of the community and the society-community relationship (Nelissen, 1972, p. 62).
c. For an economic system: producer and consumer behaviour, income and expenditure, distribution of income, allocation, influence of space and time, external effects, (international) politics and organization.

A t h e o r y is a system of statements about a part of reality. When comparing theories from different sciences it is important that these theories deal with the same aspect of reality.

Such an aspect of reality is imitated by means of m o d e l s, which form the basis of theories. The comparability of models implies, among other things, that the parameters and measuring units of those models are comparable and that they can be weighed o b - j e c t i v e l y against each other.

The differences between the subject-matters and frames of reference of ecology and economics justify the assumption that this comparability of models will be possible to a limited degree only.

3. 3. Relationships between sciences

If we wish to establish a relation between ecology and economics, there are at least four possibilities open to us. (7)

a. Reduction. A theory (T_2) from one science can be reduced to a theory (T_1) from another science if all terms of T_2 are defined by using terms of T_1 and if all the laws of T_2 can be deduced from the laws of T_1.
In view of the differences in subject-matters (see 3. 2.) the possibility of reducing economic theories to ecological theories (or vice versa) seems slight, unless one adopts some kind of 'mechanistic' standpoint.

b. Use as auxiliary science. Certain measuring units, parameters, models or theories can be extracted from one science and used in another. This use can often be converted to reduction or analogy (see below), so that it would not be logical for ecological theories to be used in economics.

c. Analogies. In an analogy it is assumed that things and/or beings from extremely different classes have similar qualities. These qualities concern both 'structure' and 'behaviour' (simulation models). Analogy (especially the simulation models) can turn out to be a useful tool in relating ecology and economics, partly because when correctly applied, no value judgments are included.

d. Synthetic models. These are models (mostly of a mathematical or statistical nature) which are built on parameters from various sciences. These sciences themselves keep 'out of range'; otherwise it would be a question of reduction, analogy or auxiliary sciences. By means of their theories or models, they supply variables which, when combined, describe reality better than they would do in each science separately. Such a synthetic (holistic) model can be regarded as a part of a master science to which certain theories of the contributing sciences could be reduced. Systems analysis is an example of such a synthetic approach (see also Keuning, 1973).

3. 4. Ecology, economics and politics

As well as discussing the methodological relationships between ecology and economics, some attention must be paid here to the way in which both sciences can function in politics, alongside or in co-operation with each other.
The actual situation reveals that on the one hand, public policy is fed by ideas, theories, facts and models from the world of science; on the other hand, politics dictates the priorities which can function within scientific models or theories. There is often a strong inter-

action between these two approaches. They will therefore be treated as o n e relationship science-politics when this seems to be useful. A policy based on integrated ecological-economic models requires objectivity in the weighing of the parameters. For a policy based on separate ecological and economic models, this is no longer required. One aspect of this is the possibility that models produce s i d e - c o n d i t i o n s with regard to matters of policy. These side-conditions can on the one hand be regarded as concrete demarcation lines (around areas), and on the other hand as abstract 'deadlines'.

3. 5. Conclusions and criteria

The foregoing enables us to make the following c o n c l u s i o n s regarding a possible combination or synthesis of ecology and economics:
- the methods of both sciences are heterogeneous, but do not exclude similarity: particularly the creation of inductive theories and empirical-scientific construction of models offer possibilities (3.1.).
- the subject-matters of both sciences overlap only slightly so that the co-operation is limited. The frames of reference have a number of themes in common, e. g. the relationship between structures in time and space, and organization. Comparability of theories and models requires means for weighing objectively (3.2.).
- 'translation' or synthesis must be effected mainly by using formal mathematical models, by means of analogies or in synthetic models (3.3.).
- ecology and economics, in certain forms and under certain conditions, can function together within the framework of a governmental policy (3.4.).
In addition to these conclusions, the e t h i c a l aspect of such a relationship should not be forgotten. Differences in subject-matter and frames of reference will have ethical implications whose effects continue to work in the use of models and parameters. Does the character of a science experience a fundamental change if its aspects are used in another? How do value judgments function within the various sciences? It is important to at least acknowledge this aspect in each relationship.
A number of c r i t e r i a can be concluded from the foregoing for models with an economic-ecological character.
1. The method used in constructing the model must be consistent; the model must describe the relevant part of reality as fully as possible.
2. The model must fall within the overlapping of subject-matters and under the regime of the common themes of the frames of reference; it must be possible to weigh the parameters objectively.
3. The system must be expressed in a formal mathematical model, an analogy of a synthetic model.

4. The ethical implications of the model must be answered for.
5. The model must include elements relevant to matters of policy.
6. The model should incorporate priorities and side-conditions
   formulated from politics unless these can be rejected from
   within the model.

Criteria 1, 2, 3 and 4 are essential for purely scientific models;
5 and 6 are of secondary importance. For decision models for
policy purposes, criteria 4, 5 and 6 are essential and 1, 2 and 3
are of secondary importance.

4. Models

In this section we will discuss a number of models and attempt to
test them by means of the above criteria. A selection did of course
have to be made. The energy theories, the Input-Output Analysis
(IOA), the Cost-Effectiveness Analysis (CEA) and the Multicriteria
Analysis (MCA) were chosen.
Other models relevant here are e. g., optimization models, damage
models, Helliwell's models (see Van der Ploeg, 1972, for this),
the Cost-Benefit Analysis (regarded here as a variant of the CEA,
namely the variant with one 'common denominator': money) and the
'materials balance' models of Ayres and Kneese (1969).

4.1. Energy theories

In 'Environment, Power and Society' (1971), H. T. Odum has tried
to describe society in its environment, the biosphere, by means of
energy-flow models, such as the energy model of a food chain:

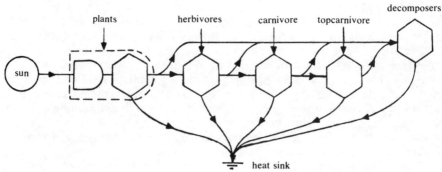

(After H. T. Odum, 1971)

Odum uses this type of diagram to describe the 'master controls' of
society: politics and religion. He also provides a number of models
for the economic system. Firstly, he considers it possible to describe energy processes in bio-ecology by using IO matrices.
These could then be compared with economic matrices. He then

defines a number of economic concepts. Some examples are:
- a g o o d is an accumulated result of useful work (its v a l u e is
  the time integral of the flow of potential energy expended in work).
- c o s t s represent the potential energy which necessarily dis-
  appears in the form of heat during a process (heat sink).
  Costs can also be seen as a current circulating in the opposite
  direction to energy.
- e c o n o m i c g r o w t h is the increase in the size of a unit of the
  system and/or its flows. It may be expressed in units of energy
  storage, or in units of value (see above).
- u n e m p l o y m e n t: circuits that have to be maintained within a
  system but are not being used for system work (e. g. reserve
  capacity or a rest period for a part of the system). Too much
  unemployment means too high 'maintenance costs'. Unemployment
  can be diminished by increasing energy outputs or by decreasing
  the population in relation to energy input.
- p r i c e s: the price for the work of an individual depends on his
  capacities to utilize available energy flows. The price of goods
  is determined by the amount of work involved, plus expenditures
  they have incurred in obtained services and materials. The price
  mechanism serves to distribute the potential energy for work
  through the system evenly.

To some extent, economic theory has been reduced to energetic
theory in these definitions. In some cases, however (Odum does
not make this sufficiently clear), analogies are present, sometimes
through simulation models. All energy models can, in turn, be
simulated by electronic connections. The energy flows can also be
described in mathematical and statistical models (see Odum, pp.
264-267 and 311-317).

Odum's ideas about economics are rather remarkable. The definitions of value, costs and prices for instance, are definitely not
in agreement with current views. Odum confines himself to the
supply side and that is of course only half of the matter. (8) The
reductions and analogies are consequently incorrect. Criteria 2
and 3 are not fulfilled.

Moreover, it seems improbable that the social (economic) activities
of man can be described sufficiently by energetic formulas (although
Odum does indeed take social ecology implicitly into account).
Consequently, criterion 4 is not satisfied either.

A different criticism is the ineffectiveness of the models. They
require an extremely large number of exactly formulated data. It
is also questionable whether a satisfactory simulation model for
social and economic processes can be given at all, since the
structure of society is much less stable than, for example, a bio-
ecosystem. Possibilities for applying Odum's theories seem therefore to occur primarily on a very small scale or in rough models
(a coupling to the systems dynamics models could offer interesting
possibilities here).

4.2. Input–Output Analysis

An Input–Output (IO) model describes how the various industries in an economy are related to each other and how they are related to the final demand for their goods. There are two objections to this method: the number of data needed is extremely large and a number of rigorous assumptions must be made. For an extensive treatment of the possibilities of an ecological-economic IO analysis, see Victor (1972). Here Isard's IO-framework will be discussed. Isard's IO model (1968), much simplified, is as follows:

		Economic activities		Ecologic processes	
		1 2 3 . . .	n	1 2 3 . . .	n
Economic commodities	1 2 3	Economic system: intersector coefficients		Ecologic processes: their input-output coefficients with regard to economic commodities	
	n				
Ecologic commodities	1 2 3 . . .	Economic sectors: their input-output coefficients with regard to ecologic commodities		Ecologic system: interprocess coefficients	
	n				

The top left-hand box is the traditional IO matrix of technical coefficients. The other boxes have been added by Isard in order to integrate ecological processes. The bottom right-hand box is an IO matrix for the complex of ecological processes. The top right-hand and bottom left-hand boxes indicate the relation between economics and ecology in coefficients. Activities and processes are both divided into n sectors each producing one type of 'good'; the commodities are divided into n columns (horizontal) each containing one commodity. Isard cites the analysis of the economic and ecological processes involving the cod-fish.

This analysis concerns a r e a s in which processes take place. However, more occurs within such an area, at least from a bio-ecological point of view, than just those processes. Criteria 1 and 2 are therefore only partly satisfied. (9)

A different objection, concerning the particular description of ecological processes (such as the food chain supporting the cod) is the impracticability of this analysis because of the very large number of data required and the immense complexity. It is therefore dubious whether such a model is really relevant to policy matters; the fulfilment of criterion 5 thus becomes doubtful.

26

4. 3. Cost-Effectiveness Analysis

In the Cost-Effectiveness Analysis (CEA) the effects of projects
are analyzed in their 'natural' dimensions when it is clear that
these effects will not be appraised in monetary terms, afterwards.
The objective of the analysis is to indicate the alternative (or
combination of alternatives) that produces either the greatest
expected effectiveness for a given expected cost, or a given expected effectiveness for the least expected cost (Seiler, 1969).
A possible procedure for this analysis includes the following steps
(Ko and Duckstein, 1972, from Kazanowski):
1. Definition of the desired objectives etc.
2. Identification of requirements needed to reach the objective.
3. Formulation of a number of alternative systems (means to
   achieve the end).
4. Determination of the evaluation criteria.
5. Assessment of the suitability of the alternatives in terms of the
   evaluation criteria.
6. Analysis of the qualities of the alternatives.
7. Sensitivity analyses (feedback).
8. Description of the whole.
The CEA is most suitable for relatively isolated projects. Moreover, the alternative systems must be independent. Dependent
alternatives can be examined in the sensitivity-analysis phase.
The number of criteria should be limited since, if there are too
many, they lose in significance. Examples of criteria are: latent
costs and benefits, factors influencing the environment, 'external
effects' in regard to the actual analysis, uncertain social factors.
The 'filling in' of non-economic criteria must be done by specialists,
by means of models from which, for example, standard levels can
be derived.
Of course, matters such as budget restrictions and boundary conditions can be included in the analysis. Kohn (1972) also states that
in the CEA voluntary co-operation is often forgotten, whereby the
'environmental goal' in the proposed solution would be more than
attained and the costs of control would not be minimum.
The presentation can vary. Ko and Duckstein (1972) who concerned
themselves with the possibility of re-using waste water and the
scarcity of pure water, present their conclusions in a table in
which the 'behaviour' of the criteria is given for each of the alternatives. The decision-maker must make his own choice although
some suggestions are made. Such an approach is described by
Opschoor and Jansen (1972) for measures concerning noise
nuisance.
Van der Meer and Opschoor (1973) suggest the application of substitution rates. They suggest three possibilities:
1. The decision-maker applies substitution rates of his own choice.
2. The analysis-maker draws up a number of sets of substitution
   rates for the decision-maker.
3. The analysis-maker fills in his own preference with regard to

the substitution rates (e.g. one of the sets referred to in 2).
A different refinement of the model is the probabilistic approach.
The 2σ isoquants for three alternatives have been set out in the
following diagram (after Seiler, 1969, p. 92):

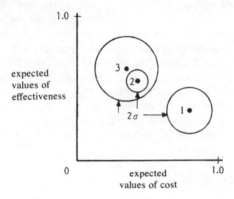

This approach reduces the chance of making a wrong decision.
The CEA is not a model which describes reality fully. The analysis
only provides arguments for the weighing of interests (Seiler, 1969,
speaks, for example, of sub-optimization). Before applying the
substitution rates, non-economic data can however, also appear
in a 'natural' way. It is, moreover, quite possible to combine all
data (if necessary in formulas) in tables and/or graphs. The CE
model is, as it were, a preliminary phase in a synthetic model:
the synthesis can be achieved by the substitutions.
Because criteria 4, 5 and 6 in particular are satisfied, the CEA
would appear to be a correct decision model which could indeed
function in the larger whole of a synthetic model.

4.4. The Multicriteria Analysis

A method which closely resembles the CEA is the Multicriteria
Analysis (MCA). This involves a selection from a finite number of
alternatives whereby an assessment is made of criteria of unequal
dimension, which one cannot or will not aggregate in one dimension.
The selection is based on the total scores of the alternatives.
One of the possible MC analyses is the Electre method, applied
among others, by Van der Meer and Opschoor (1973) and Nijkamp
(1975). This method requires:
1. A finite number of alternatives (n), assembled in the
   vector E. This means that the method is limited to conclusions
   about relative optimal solutions.
2. Criteria, or the various structures or processes which are
   affected by an alternative. The criteria must be independent and
   are assembled in the vector P.
3. A scale for each criterion, in order to classify the alternatives
   (e_1, e_2 etc.). These scales do not have to be equal for all cri-

teria. The classifications are assembled in the vector K.
4. W e i g h t s, to weigh the criteria against each other, assembled
   in vector G.
The data thus obtained are incorporated in a c o n c o r d a n c e
i n d i c a t o r (the sum of the weights of the criteria for which alternative e_i is preferred, or is equivalent to alternative e_i' divided
by the sum of all weights) and a d i s c o r d a n c e i n d i c a t o r (the
greatest difference between two criterion values of e_i and e_i', divided
by the maximal difference between two criterion values, whatever
the alternatives), which shows 'how bad' an alternative is; this requires making the various scales comparable.
With one or more sets of weights as basis and by using the indicators, it is now possible to eliminate, step by step, the less satisfactory alternatives, until one (or more!) remains. A sensitivity
analysis can be applied as a control for the variation in the weights.
The MCA used by Bertier and De Montgolfier (1973) corresponds
broadly with the above method. They call the criteria 'points of
view' and the variables which express these points of view are
called 'criteria'. The weighing of the different alternatives ('projects')
proceeds in three steps:
1. Selection of a reference criterion, depending on the given problem.
2. Weighing the other criteria against this reference. Boundary conditions can be laid down for this ratio.
3. Classification of the alternatives by a pairwise comparison. An
   'outranking relation' (strong, medium or weak) can be indicated
   for each pair.
The selection and the weighing of the criteria are of course the most
difficult phases in this method.
The MCA, like the CEA is a synthetic decision procedure. Objectives, criteria and weights are extremely important in the
analysis. The MCA is, in fact, more 'manoeuvrable' than the CEA
because economic aspects can be just as important as non-economic
aspects; accordingly, more 'questions' can be put to the analysis.
The MC model, like the CE model, is a pre-synthetic model: only
the objective weighing of the parameters against each other is
missing, so that criterion 2 is not completely satisfied. However,
because the other criteria, particularly 5 and 6 (the 'political'
criteria) are satisfied, the MCA is a good general decision model
which can offer many possibilities, with regard to scientific and
non-economic problems, as well.

5. C o n c l u s i o n s, i m p l i c a t i o n s a n d f i n a l r e m a r k s

Some conclusions and criteria concerning the scientific and political
aspects of the relationship ecology - economics were formulated
in Section 3. 5. In Section 4 we saw that none of the models examined there completely satisfied all criteria although the Cost-
Effectiveness Analysis and the Multicriteria Analysis do not come
off too badly.

This means that from the scientific point of view, the aim of a 'translation' of sciences by means of reduction or a synthetic model, has not been achieved. It is still an open question whether or not a systems approach, if practicable, could indeed lead to a synthesis between the ecological and economic sciences while still maintaining the 'special' i d e n t i t y of the component parts.

From a political point of view, a certain imperfection of decision models need not be a disadvantage. The precise weighing of interests in the CEA and the MCA will certainly produce great difficulties and contrasts even when boundary conditions are imposed. They can however, at least lead to a policy which takes many aspects of reality into account.

A comment on the function of m e r i t g o o d s is appropriate in this context. These are (individual or collective) goods (with or without external effects) which the government considers would not be consumed enough in the case of a Pareto-optimal allocation, if there were no government intervention (Edelman and Opschoor, 1970). The reverse argument applies to d e m e r i t g o o d s. The given definition implies that problems of market imperfection (including imperfect knowledge and external effects) are solved, so that intervention implies an infringement on consumer sovereignty. This is probably of interest to theoreticians but in practice there will be, at most, a sub-optimal allocation in the Paretian sense. The role of good, informative ecological-economic models with regard to collective goods is in this context tripartite. In the first place, in a sub-optimal allocation, various imperfection problems can be solved because such a model can indicate the pros and cons of certain alternatives, thus ensuring, for example, the 'perfection' of consumer knowledge. (10) Secondly, the government can, in the case of optimal allocation, on the strength of the above-mentioned models, decide to regard certain collective goods (included in those models) as merit or demerit goods. Consumer (and producer) behaviour can change because of merit qualifications. This would imply, in fact, a shift of the allocation in a sub-optimal direction! For some, our reasoning will have been too theoretic or too long. Why not regard environment as an economic good? In view of the functions of nature, (11) it would be reasonable to regard nature as a collective good. Such an approach is however too one-sided. In the first place, although 'the environment' of the bio-ecologists may be regarded as a collective good, it is very doubtful whether the human-ecological 'environment' should be characterized thus: is a human being a 'collective good'? In the second place, the qualification 'collective good' implies a certain e c o n o m i c valuation. It is this very narrowing of outlook (unless economics is an omniscience) which causes the value of many facets of the various environments to be insufficiently assessed, thus producing a distorted image of reality. A pure (welfare-) economic approach can give sufficient certainty concerning an objective weighing of possibilities and desirabilities only in cases which are very limited in time, space and variation. For that very reason, it is important that any ecological-economic models which may be made are examined closely and that possibilities for synthesis receive particular attention.

Notes

1. This article is a translation of publication no. 32 from the Institute for Environmental Studies, Free University, Amsterdam. The author acknowledges grant nrs. 46-11 and R 46-21 from the Netherlands Organization for Pure Scientific Research (ZWO).
2. See the article by Zielhuis in Oomen (1973, p. 15).
3. See the article by Nelissen in Oomen (1973).
4. This does not alter the fact that on the one hand a human-ecosystem of this type and on the other hand the systems of more highly developed cultures are dependent on bio-ecosystems to a certain extent and with regard to certain qualities only.
5. In some economic circles this empirical method causes considerable discontent, so that in recent years normative economics (as a kind of 'political economics', with econometrics as 'auxiliary science') has become more important.
6. From De Moor (1961), quoted in Nelissen (1972).
7. a., b. and c. freely adapted from Van der Steen (1971).
8. It is remarkable that although Odum's concept of value seems to be somewhat Marxistic, he regards the market mechanism as an energetic efficient principle!
9. Victor (1972, p. 46) states in this context that '... the ecologic system must be viewed in a commodity-by-process context. The industry-by-industry format .... cannot be used to describe the ecologic system'.
10. This actually seems extremely improbable: it would, for example, require a comprehensive insight into the interaction between environment and economic action and it is very doubtful if such a level of knowledge will ever be reached.
11. A survey can be found in Van der Ploeg (1972, pp. 38-39).

References

Ayres, R. U. , and A. V. Kneese, 'Production, Consumption and Externalities', Amer. Econ. Rev. LIX: 282-297, 1969.
Bertier, P. , and J. de Montgolfier, 'On Multicriteria Analysis. An application to a forest management problem'. In: Working Proceedings of the NATO-Conference: 'Mathematical analysis of decision problems in Ecology' (87-104), 1973.
Bos, P. , 'Mens-ecologie en ruimtelijke ordening; een hypothese'. In: Klaassen, L. H. (ed.), Regionale economie. Wolters-Noordhoff, Groningen (246-290), 1972.
Bouma, F. , and S. W. F. van der Ploeg, Functies van de Natuur; een Economisch-Oecologische Analyse. Institute for Environmental

Studies, Free University, Amsterdam: Publ. nr. 46, 1975.

Edelman, F. J. , and J. B. Opschoor, 'Overheid en Merit goods', Openbare Uitgaven, June 1970.

Hennipman, P. , Theorie van de economische politiek. Stenfert Kroese, Leyden, 1962.

Isard, W. , 'Some notes on the linkage of the ecologic and economic systems', Reg. Sc. Ass. : Papers XXII, Budapest Conf. : 85-96, 1968.

Kessler, A. , Een vergelijkend onderzoek naar eiproductie en nataliteit bij wolfspinnen van het genus Pardosa (Araneae, Lycosidae). Ph. D. Thesis, Free University, Amsterdam, 1973.

Keuning, D. , Algemene systeemtheorie, systeembenadering en organisatietheorie. Stenfert Kroese, Leyden, 1973.

Klant, J. J. , Spelregels voor economen. Stenfert Kroese, Leyden, 1972.

Ko, S. C. , and L. Duckstein, 'Cost-effectiveness analysis of waste water reuses', J. Sanit. Engng. Div. 98/5A6: 869-881, 1972.

Kohn, R. E. , 'Price elasticities of demand and air pollution', Rev. Econ. Statist. 54/4: 392-399, 1972.

Meer, G. J. van der, and J. B. Opschoor, Multicriteria analyse: de Electra-methode. Institute for Environmental Studies, Free Univ. , Amsterdam: Working paper nr. 17, 1973.

Nelissen, N. J. M. , Grondbeginselen van de sociale ecologie. Spectrum, Utrecht, 1972.

Nijkamp, P. , 'A Multi-Criteria Analysis for Project Evaluation', Papers of the Regional Science Association, Vol. 35, 1975, pp. 87-111.

Odum, E. P. , Fundamentals of ecology. Saunders, Philadelphia, 1971.

Odum, H. T. , Environment, Power and Society. Wiley & Sons, New York, 1971.

Oomen, H. C. J. , et al. , Mens en Ecologie. Samsom, Alphen a/d Rijn, 1973.
- R. L. Zielhuis, 'Gezondheidsecologie' (14-53).
- N. J. M. Nelissen, 'Humane ecologie' (54-94).

Opschoor, J. B. , and H. M. A. Jansen, Meten en Waarderen. Methodologische problemen bij economisch milieu-onderzoek. Institute for Environmental Studies, Free Univ. , Amsterdam: Series 'Economische Verkenningen' nr. 2, 1972.

Ploeg, S. W. F. van der, Oecologie en economie. Institute for Environmental Studies, Free Univ. , Amsterdam: Series 'Biologische Verkenningen' nr. 1, 1972.

Seiler, K. , Introduction to systems cost-effectiveness. Wiley-Interscience, New York, 1969.

Steen, W. J. van der, Wijsbegeerte van de biologie. Lecture notes, Free University, Amsterdam, 1971.

Victor, P. A. , Pollution: economy and environment. Allen & Unwin, London, 1972.

Project Evaluation and Intangible Effects: a Shadow Project Approach

L. H. Klaassen and T. H. Botterweg

1. Introduction

Many efforts made to assign values to elements of the environment have, up till now, been unsuccessful. This failure has had implications for, among other things, the development of the cost-benefit analysis, which has been increasing in importance as an instrument for project evaluation.

In order to carry out an economic analysis of several reclamation projects in the Wadden Sea area in the Netherlands which stressed in particularly the environmental effects [2] [6], it seemed advisable to set up a cost-benefit analysis which was more complete than usual and also to introduce the environmental elements in an unusual way. An analysis, where the net sum of the measurable effects is confronted with a verbal summing up of all imponderable effects, seemed, in view of the attention which the natural environment has justly been receiving the last few years, too broad as a basis for a judgement which is as objective as possible.

An approach which has recently received some attention is that of monetary compensation [1]. It is beyond the scope of this article to delve into this compensation idea because the treatment of its theoretical aspects in particular would require too much space. A few words on the subject would not be inappropriate however. Neither could we resist the temptation to expose the essential weakness of the compensation idea by giving a brief account of its background. The idea is, in principle, that when any nuisance is experienced, he who causes the nuisance should extend pecuniary compensation to him who experiences it. The latter then returns to the same state of welfare as before the nuisance was experienced.

The amount of the compensation represents, then, the assessment of the damage to the environment. A little reflection soon shows that such an approach to the matter overlooks the essence of the problem. A compensation in no way guarantees that no damage is done to the environment, whilst it is precisely this which should be the fundamental requirement of any method whatsoever. The following short narrative illustrates the situation that can occur as a result of the compensation idea.

33

There were once, not so long ago, two fathers with two sons who lived at some distance from a large town. Each of the sons had a motor bike which he had to start early in the morning in order to get to work, in town, on time. Both fathers were rudely awakened every morning by the devastating din, and even began to show signs of nervous disturbance. But, since they were wise men, they did not quarrel with each other but discussed their common problem calmly over a glass of good wine. They soon reached the conclusion however, that their own knowledge was not sufficient to solve the problem satisfactorily, and it was quite natural for them to pay a visit to the local library the very same day in order to deepen their knowledge in this field. They found an abundance of British literature which gave a detailed account of the principle of compensation. If noise nuisance was experienced, they read in profound scientific papers, monetary compensation should be given. Any deterioration in the quality of life would thus be undone.

Both men absorbed this wise advice, were completely satisfied, and acted accordingly. Over a second glass of good wine, they agreed that the value of the noise nuisance, expressed in money, would amount to about 100 pennies per day. So they arranged that the first father would pay this sum to the second father to compensate him for the annoyance caused to him by the first father's son. The second father undertook to make an offering of equal size to compensate the first father for the annoyance caused by the second father's son.

Although the noise nuisance after this agreement was no less than beforehand and their financial position was neither strengthened nor weakened, they lived together happily ever after, quite convinced that they both received full compensation for the nuisance caused to them by each other's sons. Needless to say, they now had an even deeper respect for economic science than they had, as wise men, already had.

This narrative is intended to show how little trust the authors of this article have in the compensation idea.

In its stead, another approach, that of the shadow project, seems to be more fruitful. This approach, which was originally formulated for the purpose of evaluating possible reclamations in the Wadden Sea area, can, in principle, have a much wider application within cost-benefit analysis.

We start from the assumption that nature (particularly in the Netherlands) must not be degraded any further and that it must be stipulated that for any proposed project which is detrimental to the natural environment, provision be made for the realization (or the financing) of a shadow project.

This shadow project should prevent or compensate any damage to the environment, not by means of payment of a sum of money but by an addition to the environment at least equivalent to the environmental damage incurred. The theory is that the cost-benefit analysis is not based on the value possessed by nature or the en-

vironment but on the sum of money required, i. e. the costs which
have to be made, to maintain the environment in its present state.
Although we have been discussing shadow projects as a possible
means of avoiding problems of the valuation of nature, we must
add, probably superfluously, that the shadow project concept is of
course also applicable in cases where there are imponderable
effects, e. g. of a social or cultural nature.

2. No further deterioration of nature*

In recent years, it has become increasingly apparent that natural
areas have an indispensable function within the process of town and
country planning in the Netherlands. By various regulations, the
qualification 'natural area' is made increasingly difficult to obtain,
while the purchase policy is aimed at insuring long-term preservation (including the possibility of proper control). On the other
hand the use made of natural areas has assumed such proportions
that in various instances the quality has suffered.
There are many kinds of natural areas; there are also many different reasons for a natural area to be given a protected status. Although we will not be dealing with this point in any detail, the
following brief observations may be made.
Most of the reasons are concerned with the use we can make of it,
e. g. provision of water and air, but also of foodstuffs, genes
sources and the possibility that nature signalizes poisonings etc.
Besides these resources, there is also a large group of social
motives. It can, for instance, be desirable to grant a protected
status to natural areas from an ethical or aesthetic point of view.
A richly varied nature is also of paramount importance for education
and science; science being concerned not only with nature as a
study object but also with the possibility of its use as a reference
for other studies. When enumerating the functions of the natural
environment we often tend to make an extremely long list. This
is probably justified, for there are an infinite number of reasons
for wanting a 'well functioning nature', this being, in fact directly
related to the possibility of 'life'.
It is, however, incorrect to attribute all these functions simultaneously to all natural areas - smaller or larger areas, with or without a protected status - in which the natural processes or old cultural
patterns are preserved. The functions of nature are infinite; those
of natural areas are clearly limited.
The protection of natural areas has the specific aim of preserving nature
in spite of everything. This means that the use of the natural area must
be in accordance with the specific policy principles. The purchase of a
plot of land as a breeding place for the purple heron means that it
cannot at the same time have a positive recreation value.
As we have observed previously, the valuation of functions of nature

* Credits to the co-author Mr. J.A. van der Ven.

is a risky undertaking. With natural areas it is even pointless, since the aim for which the status is granted – which may already be dubious to the outsider – indicates the value of the land. The degree to which this aim, which can materialize in a specific plan, is substantiated, will determine the value of the land. If the purpose of the natural area is of a strictly scientific kind, then this automatically determines the value. The fact that it is not given a function in the recreation sphere is a result of the specific aim and will not, therefore, have a negative influence of the assessment of the natural area.

The value of a natural area cannot, therefore, be deduced from a list of general functions of nature. There is no point in determining the extent of the contribution of o n e natural area to all the functions of nature. The value of a natural area is bound up with the proposals made for that area, these being based in particular on ecological insights.

First and foremost we must recognize that the protected natural areas in a country do not by any means represent the whole natural wealth of that country. There are, in fact, quite a lot of valuable areas which owe their character to man's differentiation of activities through the ages, up to the beginning of the twentieth century. The rich meadow bird areas, the vast moors, the pools adjoining the great rivers, the old peat diggings, the remains of primitive reclamations, etc. are undeniably the results of human activities in the past. These activities were followed however, by a natural development, in which man played an extremely modest part. There are also certain areas where man's influence has been negligible, such as coastal wetlands, estuaries, dunes and moors.

The variation in countryside to which we have become accustomed is being threatened by the adaptation to new norms and techniques. In the interest of both a 'well functioning nature' and the preservation of the greatest possible variety of natural areas and countryside, we cannot accept any further reduction of natural areas. With this in mind we will consider the following aspects in more detail.

3. Some developments in cost-benefit analysis

If in a cost-benefit analysis all the effects are discussed, then we are dealing with a s o c i a l cost-benefit analysis. In such an analysis, all social effects of a certain project for the whole community (1) are weighed against each other in order to make an assessment of the project. The principle behind such an analysis had already been accepted during the last century but, partly because of an imperfect set of instruments and incomplete statistical material could only be applied in a more or less intuitive way. The result, i. e. the ultimate assessment was, therefore, partly dependent on the qualities of the supervisor of the project, whether this was the government or a private company.

For several decades now, attempts have been made to bring certain – particularly social – imponderable effects into account in project evaluations. In some cases, efforts to quantify these effects by means of the determination of shadow prices have been successful. For some years now, there has been a growing awareness that environmental factors should also be taken into account, when space-devouring or highly polluting projects are being evaluated. Moreover, not only is increasing attention being paid to threatened biological entities and ecological processes, but it is being suggested increasingly often that certain rural and socio-cultural assets, such as unique polder (reclaimed) countryside and certain qualities of inner towns, must not automatically be sacrificed to projects which on other grounds seem acceptable. This development ensures that increasingly more aspects of our society are being included in any significant project evaluation.

In our introduction, we gave two examples of fairly recent analytic methods. We paid particular attention to the methods used to determine as objectively as possible the compensation to be paid to those incurring damage from a project.

Examples of the application of such methods are the Delta works in the Netherlands and the Third London Airport [5] [1]. In both cases, the cost-benefit analyses included the costs of financial compensation, for instance, to certain categories of fishermen, who would no longer be able to fish in the Delta area, and to those living in the neighbourhood of a new airport, who would experience noise nuisance and would therefore be obliged to move to somewhere else.

It should be apparent from the short narrative in our introduction, that these methods are unacceptable to the present authors. The reason is that when people inflict injury on each other a reciprocal compensation is useless, since it can hardly prevent any further injuries from happening. There would, at most, be something to say for this principle when there is an obvious, one-sided infliction of damage. In that case there are two possibilities. The first is that the costs to be paid for the damage are less than the costs of preventing the damage to the environment. In this case, the destruction will just continue. The second is that the price of paying for the damage is higher than the 'corrective' costs; it would then have been cheaper to prevent the damage in the first place. The method is therefore either ineffective or too expensive. If compensation is too expensive, a potential offender will presumably ensure that the damage does not occur, thus dispensing with the necessity of paying out compensation. In that case, the obligation to provide compensation has proved an effective means of preventing damage to the environment. The question then arises however: what is in fact our present relationship with the environment? The accompanying diagram is intended to illustrate that relationship.

In this diagram, the 'amount' of nature available is set out on the horizontal axis and its value per 'unit', unknown in fact, is set out on the vertical axis. The downward-sloping curve represents the 'demand' for nature. It is assumed that nature was once so abundant that the average value of a 'unit' of nature was, for man, very

'Demand' and 'supply' of nature

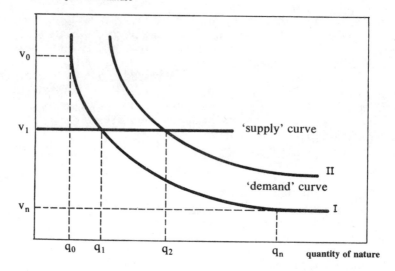

average value per 'unit' nature

small (V_n). This value remained practically the same for a long
time, until the amount of nature was depleted by deforestation and
reclamation (of waste land) to such an extent that the average
value of nature began to rise. If this development were to continue
further, then the time would come when there is so little nature
left (q_0) that its value is extremely high (V_0). Each further decrease of nature results in an even more rapid increase in value.
The value will finally become infinitely high.
It is clear that in this last stage a monetary compensation for the
detrimental effects of a certain project is no longer possible.
Every project involving environmental damage becomes socially
unremunerative.
In the following, we will be assuming that in the western world,
and certainly in the Netherlands, apart from certain local or
regional exceptions, we have reached a point on the demand curve
that corresponds with an amount of nature q_1 : nature has become
so scarce that we do not appear to be very far from the point at
which the value of nature becomes infinite.
The ever increasing number of efforts to prevent a further decrease
in the amount of nature and even to enlarge this amount indicate
that we have now reached the point q_1 . This would mean that we
have already overstepped a certain mark and that a greater 'amount'
of the good 'nature' is generally considered to be desirable.
If we imagine a horizontal supply curve through V_1, which means
that we are capable of 'producing' nature at a cost per unit of V_1,
then a further encroachment on nature from that point would be

societally pointless. This is because the value lost is greater than the cost of avoiding the damage or providing compensation in some other way by means of e f f e c t i v e measures.

An increasing appreciation of nature will reveal itself in an upward movement of the demand curve. The amount of nature required will then increase and the supply curve will intersect the demand curve at a point more to the right. This means that the cultivation of nature becomes a socially significant matter until point q_2 on the horizontal axis is reached. A downward shift of the supply curve means an increase in knowledge about and efficiency of 'nature cultivation'. Since the value of nature is not known, but the fact that no further damage to nature will be permitted i s, we will assume in the following that the point of intersection of demand and supply curves has been reached (or perhaps even passed) and for that reason, compensation i n n a t u r a will have to be given for every imminent infringement.

4. The shadow project and the project evaluation

Because of the limitations of the methods of cost-benefit analysis discussed in the previous section, and the view that we have, at least in the Netherlands, arrived at a situation in which the amount of nature has reached or passed its lowest level, a summary of the shadow project idea will now be presented. (2)
Suppose we are to evaluate a proposed project which has on the one hand certain technico-economic and social advantages and dis-advantages and on the other hand certain environmental disad-vantages. It is of course quite conceivable that the project is en-vironmentally neutral or that its effects on the environment are positive. We will return to these positive effects later on.
Suppose also that both the technico-economic and the social effects are positive and when combined have a volume of $(dT + dS)$. (3)
It is not just enough for this sum of net effects $(dT + dS)$ to be positive. If the project - excluding environmental effects for the moment - is to be profitable, then its investment and other costs (C) must be offset. The following must therefore apply:

$$dT + dS = KC \qquad \text{where } K \geq 1 \qquad (4.1)$$

In this equation, K is the socio-economic benefit-cost ratio.
If the sum of the net effects of the project $(dT + dS)$ as well as the investment and other costs are now known, then the socio-economic benefit-cost ratio can be determined, the criterion being that this ratio is at least equal to unity, since the project would not other-wise be profitable.
However, the fact that the project will encroach on nature to a certain degree (dN) has yet to be taken into account. Therefore, instead of (4.1), the following equation should be applicable:

$$dT + dS + dN = K*C \qquad \text{where } K* \geq 1 \qquad (4.2)$$

If K* - the social benefit-cost ratio, with a wider scope than K -
were measurable, then we could ascertain whether or not the project is
socially profitable. Damage to the environment is however not quantifiable, and K* is therefore not measurable. Thus, no conclusion
can be made regarding the social productivity of the project.
The following solution, already hinted at in the foregoing and based
on the assumption that the environment must not be spoiled any
further, now becomes possible. This means that one or more shadow
projects, whose task it is to remove or avoid those consequences
of the project which are detrimental to the environment should be
carried out at the same time as the original project, desired on
economic and social grounds. Since dN = 0 in that case, given the
costs of these shadow projects, we can calculate K* in (4.2). Investment and other costs involved in the shadow projects are added
to the investment costs of the project in this calculation. Total investment costs are therefore higher, and the unavoidable result is
that K* < K. The social benefit-cost ratio of the project will therefore be lower than the socio-economic benefit-cost ratio. Only if
the project does not have any environmental effects will K = K*.
In sum, the foregoing implies that, if a project has adverse effects
on the natural environment, these disadvantages will have to be
compensated by executing shadow projects simultaneously. As a
result of this action however, the socio-economic profitability of
the basic project will become lower than when there is no need to
carry out shadow projects, because the costs of the shadow projects
have to be charged to the basic project.
If we apply the shadow-project idea, we clearly reduce the problem
of quantifying the non-quantifiable. Moreover, since the non-
quantifiable detrimental effects are offset by shadow projects, the
greatest possible care is taken that nature is not spoiled any
further, or in any case that the loss is replaced as much and as
well as possible. The use of the shadow-project idea in the cost-
benefit analysis represents, therefore, an improvement on the
method of monetary compensation discussed earlier, which could
not guarantee that the expected damage would be removed. Perhaps
needlessly, we repeat that the shadow-project idea was not just
devised as an analytical instrument and that shadow projects should
be set up as compensation for certain losses.
Three additional remarks form a fitting conclusion to this section.
Firstly, it is of course not essential that the supervisor of the
initial project undertakes the shadow project as well. In many
cases that could even be undesirable, particularly if the basic
project and the shadow project are of such different characters
that it is impossible for one supervisor to have insight into the
specific problems attached to the execution of both projects. It is
of course essential that the promoter of the initial project provide
the finances necessary for the execution of the shadow project(s)
accompanying this initial project.

Secondly, we could question the soundness of our basic assumption. Is it correct to contend that, in the Netherlands at least, nature must not be spoiled any further? In Section 2 we have attempted to show that this assumption is justified.

The concern shown by experts such as biologists and ecologists for the environment could even arouse the impression that too much nature has been lost already, so that even shadow projects 'in arrears' would have to be carried out. This would imply that in future every project with effects detrimental to the environment should be accompanied by the appropriate shadow projects.

In the Netherlands such a shadow project 'in arrears' has already been proposed in one instance. Conservators have declared themselves in favour of the realization of a new sand bar with dunes and a briny pool off the Voorne coast, to compensate for the recent loss of the natural area 'De Beer'. This natural area was sacrificed to the construction of Europoort, the new seaport area near Rotterdam. If such a harbour project had been submitted for approval today, instead of 10 years ago, then 'De Beer' would at least have had to be replaced by an equivalent - newly created - natural area. This would have been a good example of a shadow project!

Our last comment is of a more general nature. We must not forget that the shadow-project idea is not necessarily concerned only with the avoidance of damage to nature or the replacement of nature which has been destroyed, but can also be concerned with, for example, the preservation of old town centres, the preservation of rural scenery, the avoidance of noise nuisance to man, in short the preservation of all sorts of cultural, natural, social and even technico-economic entities - such as windmills and other old industrial establishments - which for the sake of new projects are threatened by destruction. They are in danger of being sacrificed not exactly because one forgets to include such impending losses in the evaluation, but rather because they are often so difficult to quantify that one is wary of including them. We have already shown that the shadow-project idea can be of great help here since, instead of including in the calculations the value of what has been lost, the cost of avoiding the loss or of replacing it can be added to the cost of the proposed project.

5. The problem of the non-interchangeability of shadow projects

In the foregoing, we have avoided giving a definition of a shadow project, since we are faced with an almost endless number of possible ways of spoiling the natural environment.

A requirement of a shadow project designed to replace nature which has been lost to us is that the replacement resemble the original as closely as possible. In view of the numerous possible ways of spoiling nature, it is obvious that this requirement can cause problems. It is hardly possible, certainly for economists, to predict the problems

related to the specification of a suitable series of shadow projects pertaining to a specific project. We believe, however, that in practice, there will indeed be possibilities of defining the environmental damage as accurately as possible and then finding suitable shadow projects. The nature of the shadow project is of course closely bound up with the nature of the environmental damage. In order to define our views in more detail, it seems sensible to classify all possible kinds of environmental degradation under a number of main headings. We distinguish, among others:
1. noise nuisance,
2. air pollution,
3. water pollution (by both solid and liquid wastes; thermic pollution),
4. surface pollution,
5. visual 'pollution',
6. the loss of natural areas as well as the excessive frittering of these areas.

It is clear that for each of these groups of infringements, choosing one or more shadow projects requires a different approach. For each group we will now indicate briefly, using some simple examples, which shadow projects could be considered as possibilities.

Ad 1. If the production of sound causes damage to the environment (for instance by disturbance to people or by disturbance of a bird sanctuary) the only solution seems to be to specify a shadow project in such a way that the expected noise nuisance is avoided or is rendered harmless.

It is for instance conceivable that if a motorway is to be constructed in a sound-sensitive area, sound absorbent installations (e. g. an earth bank) be built at the side of the motorway. If this is not possible then this particular motorway must be projected farther away from this area. The higher investment costs which this requires come under the costs of the shadow project and should therefore be paid by the initiator of the project.

The shadow project attached to noise nuisance caused by aeroplanes is made up of two elements; a restriction of flying and the use of low-noise motors. Here too, the cost of the shadow project consists of the resulting extra costs for the airline companies and their passengers.

Ad 2. It is difficult to imagine that an air-purifying installation would be projected away from the source of pollution as compensation for a certain degree of air pollution. At specific points in different towns, where traffic causes an excess of air pollution however, they are being tested.

If we wish to eliminate the problem of air pollution by shadow projects, then elimination at the source of pollution - i. e. an 'avoiding' shadow project - seems a good solution. All sorts of filter systems have been and are being designed to limit air pollution. The problem is, however, that the air pollution caused by, for example, an industrial process, can never be 100 per cent eliminated. Moreover, with continually improving purification, marginal costs rise with increasing speed.

If a certain level of air pollution must not be exceeded and a certain new activity can purify only 80 per cent of its emission, then the remaining 20 per cent will have to be taken care of by a further limitation of air pollution of the same kind in other activities, until this 20 per cent is compensated.

Certain injustices are probably unavoidable here - should one activity have to purify more than other, older, activities? Problems concerning the 'import' and 'export' of air pollution will also arise. Assessment of the costs of purification, if and as much as possible, seems the appropriate solution here.

Ad 3. The specific problems attached to air pollution, arising from the non-local character of this form of pollution, apply in many cases to water pollution also. The most important difference is that, contrary to polluted air, polluted water can be collected at a central point. The purification of water can therefore occur away from the source of pollution.

As was the case with air pollution - and surface pollution (ad 4) - shadow projects for water-polluting processes should be sought in the form of a v o i d a n c e of damage.

Ad 5. It is difficult to estimate the extent to which visual pollution is detrimental to nature. (4) Visual pollution does of course infringe upon the possibilities of enjoying nature. Shadow projects can also be defined for visual pollution, aiming at avoidance of disfiguration. It is, for example, possible to lay high voltage cables underground. Although this is of course relatively expensive.

An increasingly intensive search is being made for ways of avoiding disfiguration of the countryside by elements such as cooling towers, switch stations etc. They could, for instance, be constructed underground, camouflaged by green belts or given an attractive exterior. Once again the costs of the damage-avoiding shadow projects have to be added to the costs of the initial project.

Ad 6. While the shadow projects related to the above pollution categories had a damage- a v o i d i n g character, it is conceivable that, if natural areas are threatened (with destruction) as a result of a certain project, the corresponding shadow projects should have a r e p l a c i n g character.

Before considering these r e p l a c i n g shadow projects further, we will first give some examples of this type of shadow project. A motorway which has been projected through a natural area, not only reducing the total area but also dividing it into two smaller parts, could be made to go around the natural area and not through it. Sea defences are often improved by straightening out sea dikes. Because of the lower investment costs, this is usually done on the sea side. The obvious objection to this is that natural areas, such as mud flats, are thereby threatened with destruction. The dikes can, however, also be straightened on the landward side in order to preserve the mud flats. An objection to this alternative approach is that land must be expropriated, and that certain areas of cultivated land threaten to become isolated and are not well-protected against floods. The costs of remedying these drawbacks should therefore be regarded as the costs of the shadow project.

In some cases it will be quite impossible to find a d a m a g e - a v o i d i n g shadow project for a certain basic project. The shadow project will then have to be of the r e p l a c i n g kind. An example of such a basic project is the construction of Europoort near Rotterdam, previously referred to, which necessitated the sacrifice of the natural area 'De Beer'. As we have already noted, a (partial) replacement of De Beer off the Voorne coast is now being considered. This project can be regarded as a typical replacing shadow project.

Because of their unique character, certain natural elements are irreplaceable. It would be correct to decide in such cases, proceeding on the assumption that no further degradation of nature may be allowed to occur, that however urgent the initial project, a natural area of this kind must not be sacrificed. Higher investment (or exploitation) costs will have to be accepted so that the project can be realized elsewhere - i.e. on a less suitable site.

If the natural objects involved are not, in principle, irreplaceable, shadow projects can certainly be defined to replace that nature which has been lost as a result of the construction of the initial project. In many countries where a large proportion of 'nature' is not really nature since it arose in the past largely as a result of human actions, it seems quite conceivable that large sections of this nature are replaceable.

A b i o l o g i c a l p o l i c y concerned with the replacement of existing nature has, however, one noteworthy aspect. It takes time to make 'nature'. A new natural area often takes many decades and perhaps even centuries to develop into a stable system. Moreover, developments of this kind should, particularly at the outset, be accompanied by (costly) measures of control. The drawback that there is a period of many years during which the nature that has been sacrificed no longer exists and the nature replacing it is not yet available should not be forgotten in the evaluation. Determining the extent of this drawback produces difficulties, since it is impossible to give an opinion on the value of nature. (5)

This is not, however, the greatest problem. Although the transition period can be lengthy, the requirement that nature is not endangered in the long run will in any case be satisfied. The most important problem is the design of suitable replacing projects. The problem of the valuation of nature in money terms would seem to present itself again here. The difference with the money compensation idea, however, lies in the fact that in the shadow project approach it suffices to define a shadow project corresponding in value to nature which has been lost, while in the compensation idea a valuation in money of that which has been lost would have been necessary. This means that solving the problem is simplified by replacing the need for a quantification by that for a classification of values.

There is a general rule that for each basic project for which only shadow projects with a replacing character come into consideration, a large number of possibly suitable shadow projects must be designed which may be used to replace, wholly or partially, nature that has been lost to us. From these, ecologists and others can choose those projects which between them provide just enough compensation for the nature which is to be sacrificed. This group of shadow projects should of course be chosen in such a way that the total cost remains as low as possible.

It appears, therefore that possibilities for defining shadow projects of a replacing character do indeed exist. However, since the specification of suitable replacing shadow projects will be a difficult and lengthy procedure, it seems desirable to introduce a supplementary requirement. This is that shadow projects with an avoiding character should take priority over shadow projects with a replacing character unless avoidance involves so much money and effort that these costs are higher than those of replacing shadow projects.

Only when it appears that neither avoidance nor replacement is possible, will we be unable to satisfy the basic requirement that nature must not be spoiled any further. The question whether the project under consideration is so urgent that it should be carried out in any case should be answered within the framework of the democratic decision-making process.

6. Some supplementary comments

Some comments to supplement the foregoing seem to be appropriate here.

Firstly, it should be emphasized that a project which has features which are detrimental to the environment can also have features which are favourable to the environment. It is, for instance, conceivable that although the construction of a new road from A to B results in an increase of road traffic from A to B, thus causing extra air pollution, the new connecting road is not only shorter but has abolished traffic congestion. The increase in air pollution as a result of the preference for the new road instead of, for instance, the train, is counterbalanced by a decrease in air pollution due to a more efficient traffic flow. In this case, compensation by means of a shadow project only has to be provided for the net increase in air pollution. (6)

A second example is concerned with replacing shadow projects. If during the construction of an open-air recreation area a part of the natural environment has been violated, but has been replaced according to the requirements described earlier, then over-compensation could arise, e. g. if the recreation project itself possesses natural qualities. This is quite conceivable because open-air recreation areas are often laid out in a more or less 'natural' way, so that when the trees and shrubs are full-grown and when extensive recreative use has been made of parts of the recreation area, 'nature' can arise. This nature can only be called over-compensating if the condition laid down earlier that this new nature be equivalent to the value of the (part of) nature that has been destroyed, is satisfied. In that case, provision for the new nature can be taken account of in the definition of the shadow projects of the initial recreation project in such a way that no over-compensation takes place. Thus, a saving in the investment costs of the shadow projects will be effected.

It is possible that the new nature mentioned in the previous example is n o t of the same kind as the nature which has been lost. This takes us on to the following point. If we require that nature is not depleted any further but do not require at the same time that nature must if possible be extended, it could possibly represent a saving in costs if shadow projects were designed for g r o u p s of initial projects. The theory is that the over-compensation resulting from a certain project can be used as a shadow project for another project, if the kind of nature that is over-compensated is appropriate.

Although this view places high demands on the exchange of information, it is conceivable that a central controlling organ, probably necessary anyhow for the assessment and approval of combinations of initial project ⟷ shadow projects, could also function as a 'shadow-project bank'. Over-compensations of completed projects are 'stored' here and if possible brought out again to serve as a shadow project of other projects. All this would of course be accompanied by a monetary clearance, which would also proceed through the shadow-project bank. An advantage of such a system is that there is no discrimination between individual enterprises and the government. With an internal clearance of shadow projects pertaining to governmental initial projects, the government could have the advantage over individual enterprises. Since an individual enterprise is concerned with only one or few initial projects it will have no or few possibilities of exchanging shadow projects.

Another possibility presented by a shadow-project bank is the clearance of other advantages which shadow projects offer. A shadow project which serves to create nature can, for example, offer both social and economic benefits simultaneously. These benefits can then again be included among the benefits of the basic project or can compensate the social and economic disadvantages of other projects, if these are of the same kind as the extra social and economic benefits of the shadow project in the environmental sphere.

Another problem is that although we have continually been assuming that there are still 'voids' where the shadow project can be realized, this is true to a very limited degree only. New sandbanks which rise out of the sea or new islands which are growing slowly in the

Wadden Sea are indeed areas which can replace land which has been forfeited elsewhere. In most other cases, we will not be able to find land where there is 'nothing'. Many of these areas, which we have indicated above by the term 'natural area' may have a completely natural vegetation but can also have an old agrarian structure. According to the earlier formulation of our basic assumption in this article, such areas of land are not suitable as sites for a shadow project because they do not add to the amount of nature already available. Even so, a somewhat less narrow interpretation of the term 'shadow project' is possible. We could say that the extension of a good protective status to areas which are threatened with destruction, or the avoidance of a seemingly unavoidable menace to an area, can also be regarded as a project in the sense described above.

For instance, if the construction of a very controversial road can no longer be avoided, compensation could be found by cancelling a connection somewhere else, sound in itself, but just as harmful. This kind of compensation can solve the problem of no land being available for the realization of shadow projects.

One last comment remains to be made. As we have suggested above, the shadow-project idea can also be applied to other non-quantifiable values. This application makes sense if rare things are involved, which are faced with imminent destruction if certain new projects are carried out.

One of the most spectacular examples of this is the construction of the Assuan Dam. Expensive operations were carried out to spare historical buildings or to remove them elsewhere.

Here too, the shadow projects must be of the same nature as the objects that have been lost to us. Here too, we can consider both avoiding and replacing shadow projects.

An example of an avoiding shadow project is the construction of an underground railway along a financially less favourable route so that a certain asset will not have to be spoiled. The reconstruction (perhaps elsewhere) of a valuable property is an example of a replacing shadow project. This reconstruction should take place in appropriate surroundings.

7. Conclusion

The shadow project idea is founded on the non-quantifiability of certain values. Because of this non-quantifiability, not every project which is accompanied by certain negative external effects is tested exhaustively for its social productivity. If they had indeed been tested, many projects which have been given the green light in the past, would have been rejected. No-one can be blamed for past mistakes. Instruments for determining the social effect of all kinds of human activities did not even exist at the time the decisions were made.

In our opinion, the shadow project concept creates a possibility of evading the decay of all sorts of assets. If we are really concerned about our environment in the broadest sense of the word, application of the shadow project concept can certainly provide a way out.

This means however that more exacting demands will have to be made on every project with external effects. Either the project will become less profitable because extra investments will be needed to avoid certain effects, or it will become less productive because the investment costs of shadow projects to be carried out to replace certain forfeited values have to be included in the costs of the basic project.

The price of caring about a really acceptable social development is, therefore, that projects involving extensive external effects - in relation to the other advantages and disadvantages of the project - will not be chosen. If we are indeed prepared to pay this price then the shadow-project idea can, as we have already seen, be the answer. In that case it would be worth-while developing this idea in more detail as soon as possible, paying particular attention to the problem of defining shadow projects. For this purpose, we could, for example, take a number of test objects and at the same time carry out a complete cost-benefit analysis which includes the shadow projects that will have to be carried out. If such a test were in any way successful, then we should have moved a step forward in the direction of a more acceptable society.

Notes

1. Effects which influence not only the national community but also the international community come into mind here.
2. Readers are referred to titles nr. 3, 4 and 6 on our reference list for a more detailed account.
3. dT represents the net change in technico-economic capital and dS a change in social capital, both occurring as a result of the project.
4. Visual pollution, formed for instance by old buildings may sometimes be a help to nature, since they provide homes for animal species such as bats and barn owls.
5. The longer the transition period, the more difficult it can be for flora and fauna threatened with extinction to acclimatize to the new, specially adapted, environment.
6. This applies only if one's aim is the elimination of any further increase in air pollution. If one's objective is more stringent then m o r e than the net increase of air pollution should be eliminated.

References

1. Commission on the Third London Airport; Papers and Proceedings; inter alia vol. VII, par. 20. 3, p. 366.

2. Klaassen, L. H. , and T. H. Botterweg, 'Evaluating a Socio-Economic and Environmental Project', Papers of the Regional Science Association, vol. 33, 1974, pp. 155–175.
3. Klaassen, L. H. , and J. H. P. Paelinck, 'Maatschappelijke Baten-Kosten Analyses; enkele Kwalitatieve Beschouwingen', in: Economie dezer Dagen, Rotterdam University Press, Rotterdam, 1973.
4. Klaassen, L. H. , and A. C. P. Verster, assisted by T. H. Botterweg, Kosten-Baten Analyse in Regionaal Perspectief. Tjeenk Willink, Groningen, 1974.
5. Tinbergen, J. , De Economische Balans van het Deltaplan, Report Delta Commission, 1960.
6. Report Wadden Sea Commission, 1974.

Environmental Administration, Economic-Spatial Structure and Physical Planning

J. G. Lambooy

1. Environmental problems and the spatial structure of economic activity

In this chapter we will be considering two problems. We intend to investigate:
1. the extent to which the various environmental issues are related to the spatial structure; and also
2. the extent to which the problem of the environment can be solved through physical planning (i. e. aiming at a different spatial structure).

Human existence requires the use of other forms of life - such as plants and animals - and of space. This can easily lead to a competitive situation and can even end up in dislodgment or destruction of these other forms of life.

Man himself is, however, in his use of environment and space first and foremost a biotic and physical being. He needs the 'input' of nutritive matter extracted directly from raw materials (perhaps artificially, for example via chemical industries) or via the plant and animal world. Man also wants to be clothed and housed, which involves calling upon the a-biotic part of nature as well. Hereby, one must take into account that every activity requires an input of space. On the 'output' side there is also some space occupation as well. The above statement applies therefore to both producer and consumer activities.

We can divide the products of human activities into three groups:
1. investment or capital goods - used to ensure production continuity;
2. consumer goods - for the direct satisfaction of human needs;
3. 'waste' - including that which is released during the production process and that which is released through consumption: for instance, nitrogen oxides during the production of electricity and noise through the consumption of pop music from a transistor radio on a crowded beach.

We have just made the assertion that on both input and output sides, all activities need 'space'. The space occupied does of course differ for each activity. In prehistoric times, hunters often needed several square kilometers per caput as hunting grounds in order to survive. In modern times, considerably less space is sufficient for a farmer to produce the same amount of food. Human progress shows that the minimum space per caput physically necessary for survival has decreased considerably. Population density (i. e. the number of people per surface unit) was able to increase greatly as our technical knowledge increased. In principle, the expectation is that developments in technique will probably lead to another considerable increase in density over the whole world and will also enable us to guarantee a better life for an even greater number of people.

This view should, however, be tested differently in different regions, since as soon as we start to differentiate spatially, we perceive that the age-old trend towards a decline in space occupation per inhabitant has in many areas changed into a tendency towards an i n c r e a s i n g space occupation. This will obviously occur in those areas where:

a. urbanization is in a very advanced stage, and

b. money income per caput is high,

since these are the areas where we find a high density of motor cars, infrastructure and capital-intensive enterprises. (1)

In this analysis, we should, however, make a distinction between d i r e c t and i n d i r e c t space occupation of activities. The space occupied by an activity can be described as the exclusive or competitive use of a part of 3-dimensional space; involving of course not only the surface, but the height and volume as well. D i r e c t s p a c e o c c u p a t i o n refers to the direct use of space for a certain activity, such as for instance, an office building with its own parking area. We speak of i n d i r e c t s p a c e o c c u p a t i o n when the spatial effects do not occur in the same place but elsewhere, such as when the construction of a block of flats is completed elsewhere by the construction of playing fields, roadways and a sewage purification plant. Obstruction of the view we could perhaps call indirect space occupation or subjective space occupation. We could also use the terms p r i m a r y and s e c o n d a r y (or derived) space occupation.

It is important to emphasize that the economically relevant activities, production and consumption, are practically always related to a specific place, via an 'establishment' (or site). (Settlement and establishment are terms also used in Social Geography). The nature of the activities and therefore the nature of the establishment determine at the same time the character of the space occupation.

For our purposes, we distinguish three types of establishment:

1. E n t e r p r i s e s with profit (income) objectives (such as refineries, engineers' bureaux, medical doctors, theatres, hotels).

2. I n s t i t u t i o n s aimed at rendering services (schools, hospitals, churches, governmental offices, registrated offices of associations.

3. D w e l l i n g s.

There are also certain structures which are not directly characteristic of present-day activities, e. g. windmills, castles etc. which can be indicated by the term m o n u m e n t s. The spatial expression of the relations between the above three establishments among others can be found in particular in the phenomenon traffic and transport.

A fairly high spatial concentration of establishments is essential for modern society. In both extremely sparsely populated countries such as Australia and Canada (seen as a whole) and densely populated Northwest Europe, a high percentage of the population is urbanized. The density ratios for urbanized areas between Australia, Canada and the Netherlands etc. do not therefore differ as much as is sometimes suggested. It is incorrect to use total density figures, at least for our purposes.

Modern technical development and economic and cultural advantages encourage, in general, spatial aggregation. The density of the urbanized zones in the economically developed countries increases automatically for this reason. The concept 'density' is, however, relative. A b s o l u t e d e n s i t y (the number of people per surface unit) should really be related to time as well as to space. Phenomena such as commutation cause the density in urban areas to differ during the day and night. 'R e l a t i v e d e n s i t y ' can therefore be defined as 'the number of people, per surface unit, per unit of time'. This enables a deeper insight into the p r e s s u r e on space - a figure of 1,000 inhabitants per km^2 does not tell us enough by itself, especially when we are dealing with smaller areas, such as sections of cities. The speed of locomotion is also important. Whether these people travel on foot or by car makes a great difference to the way they experience the density - the chance of an encounter or a collision increases exponentially if the speed of locomotion increases. A decrease in the maximum possible density then follows.

Not only absolute and relative density but also the e x t e n t o f t h e i n t e r r e l a t i o n s between the establishments within an area is important for concentration and space occupation. This relationship can arise in three ways:
1. through the mutual supply of goods, work or information;
2. through contact with a c o m m o n s u p p l i e r or c u s t o m e r;
3. through connections with c e r t a i n p h y s i c a l e l e m e n t s, such as the establishment of an office in a neighbourhood with 'status buildings' or of an industry near a mine or a deep sea port (cf. external effects, 'spin-off' and 'spill-over' effects).

In modern urbanized areas there is a very close relation between the establishments, with or without the benefits and drawbacks of agglomeration. The consequence of this phenomenon and the other factors which affect space occupation is that man has changed his environment to the extreme. The complex of interrelated establishments needs an enormous supply of raw materials imported from elsewhere (food, apparatuses, energy) and yet they then export other goods and services. These flows are however only part of the total 'material balance' of a city district. Within the area itself there are often activities involving the extraction of, for instance, water and sand from the earth while on the other hand huge masses of gases, noise and waste are 'produced', part of which is also 'exported' to surrounding regions. In these areas man has created a completely new ecosystem; one evolving around human needs. Flora and fauna have been drastically affected. Many varieties have disappeared and others have been introduced by man himself, wittingly or unwittingly.

The central theme of our chapter is now whether or to what extent these man-made spatial structure and processes determine the problem of the environment and whether it is possible, by choosing a different spatial structure, i. e. a different spatial organization of the establishments and activities described above (by physical planning) to provide a solution for this problem. We will now try to show that:
1. an essentially different spatial structure is, with the present social and economic relationships, not really possible;
2. the problems can indeed in the long run be partly solved by physical planning but within a shorter period can only be marginally solved (we shall be considering Mishan's proposition regarding 'separate facilities': see Mishan, 1967 and 1968); and
3. the real solution must be sought particularly in the development of technical knowledge, change of processes and products and in a different and lower production and consumption level, as well as in a change of mentality, which we will not go into.

Before we analyse these problems further, it would be useful to define more fully the concepts of spatial structure and physical planning.

The concept 'spatial structure' can be defined as a more or less permanent constellation of relations between spatial elements (mostly activities and establishments). Two types of relations can be distinguished:
1. communicative relations, such as transport, exchange of ideas etc. ; and
2. non-communicative relations, such as prohibitions, regulations, relationships, locational coupling etc. (these forms of relation can also be indicated by terms such as contact relations, institutional relationships and emotional ties.

The first type includes spatial processes which occur within the structure, such as, for example, migration and communication and which do not alter the structure itself (or only in the very long run). A change in the spatial structure as such, mostly caused by or through the non-communicative relations is of course also accompanied by spatial processes especially in the long run. The 'translation' of spatial structures and processes onto the chart produces spatial patterns which give as it were a spatial cross section of a process in time.

The concept of physical planning can be defined as an instrument used by the government to steer the spatial structure or spatial order and the spatial processes in the direction it desires. Opportunities to change are of course extremely limited: in general, all structures resist change; this is particularly true of spatial structures. The period of changeability, together with physical and economic factors, are of importance.

The extent to which the use of space can be controlled by the government, as the representative of the public interest, depends to a large degree on the extent to which the spatially relevant activities can be influenced - or in the economic sense: the activities of producers and consumers. In our society these are related to each other in the first place via the market, with prices as signals for and of the transactions and decisions.
What does the government do now, in an e c o n o m i c s e n s e, if it uses physical planning as a measure?
When answering this question, it is wise to maintain the traditional distinction between the relevant factors:
1. those which are included among the m a r k e t q u a n t i t i e s; and
2. those which are included among the d a t a (marginal conditions or exogenous conditions) for the transactions of market participants.
A clear distinction between the two is of course not always possible, but it can nevertheless be of service in the analysis of governmental measures and their effects. Measures by the government can therefore be active both via the market and via the data. These can be specified as follows:

I. Market

A. Demand and supply r a t i o s and p r i c e s of
   a. production factors (including land and raw materials);
   b. intermediate goods;
   c. final goods.
B. Transport costs in relation to the relative location.
C. The price level, arising from institutional factors, but still strongly influenced by market demand and supply, thus enabling differences to occur in the prices which, according to A, would arise (e. g. agricultural prices, collective wage agreements).

II. Data

a. the p r e s e n c e and q u a l i t y of production factors;
b. the regional cultural pattern (climate of labour, religion, level of education, consumer preferences etc.);
c. legal institutions (the organization of the market, as expressed by the competitive policy (collective wage agreements, legal regulations regarding physical planning, environment etc.);
d. infrastructure:

1. physical infrastructure (ports, roads);
2. cultural infrastructure and medical infrastructure (hospitals, schools);

e. technical knowledge;
f. information and communications (presence of clubs and lobby, stock exchange and banks etc.);
g. capacity of the environment and degree of pollution; and also, to a certain extent,
h. home and recreational environment.

One of the reasons for the importance of the distinction is the difference in level between the decisions about both groups of data. Decisions concerning data are in general taken at a higher level than those concerning the market. It is therefore useful to describe the decisions concerning the data, 'system determining': we then speak of a system determining decision level. This thought, although in a different form, is traditional in economic theory. We refer the reader to the standard work on this by Eucken (1965). It seems the right moment to assume that, with regard to our subject, physical planning influences, in particular, the behaviour of producers and consumers, via the data. There is hardly any direct intervention at the institutional decision level, (enterprises, family households). (2) This implies that with regard to the problem of the environment there is no intervention through physical planning in the action itself. In economic policy, this happens more often, for example when the price policy or a policy of quotas is used to influence market transactions. It would of course be possible to support the view that this is, ultimately, an intervention via the data. The gap between both cannot be clearly defined and is partly dependent on the time perspective. If we regard Categories I and II as, respectively, endogenous and exogenous quantities, then we could, as Tinbergen and Lerner have done, create a 'political' and an 'analytic' or 'instrumental' problem. For example, which prices etc. are necessary to achieve a certain spatial constellation and environmental situation? Physical planning operates on a long-term basis and belongs unmistakably to operating through data. For its use, however, we need a clear insight into the degree to which spatial structure and environmental problems are interrelated. We will therefore go into this problem more deeply before discussing physical planning as an instrument to be used in environmental control.

2. Environment and space

We can roughly distinguish three types of environmental problems:
1. the Club of Rome type of problem: an 'all' inclusive analysis of the inter-relationships between population, use of raw materials, pollution etc.;
2. conservation of flora, fauna and the countryside;

3. the pollution problem – of air, surface, water, noise and solid
   waste.
We are primarily concerned here with groups 2 and 3 and their
relationships with the spatial structure.

C o n s e r v a t i o n implies that:
a. the u s e of a certain territory is limited or absolutely prohibited;
b. its maintenance is aimed as much as possible at preserving it in
   its characteristic situation.
There is no doubt that the pressure to give this type of valuable
territory an alternative use will be especially strong where
establishments of economic activities are sited nearby and in great
density, particularly in and around the larger city districts. Here
especially, land is extremely scarce and there is only much too
often keen competition between conservation and allocation for activities such as industry, housing, recreation and traffic. If the
market mechanism can operate freely, or there is a high level of
unemployment or housing shortage, conservation will more than
likely not be chosen.
We should emphasize however, the subsequent tension in our affluent
society. An interesting aspect is that the increase in average income
can actually cause two contradictory effects to occur:
1. on the one hand, because of the increased use of motor cars,
   desire for larger living space, more swimming pools etc. , the
   demand for land increases, particularly (see above) in and
   around the large city districts; and
2. on the other hand, the appreciation of natural areas rises, so
   that the scarcity and its social value rise, thus causing the
   possibility of 'political' counterpressure to the demand for reallocation of land use to become greater.
The nature of the relevant area is clearly important here. 'Pure'
natural areas, being very scarce, will be irreplaceable within the
city districts; replacement can only occur by retreating to more
distant areas and this is of course not really replacing but only
shifting visits or use elsewhere.
The total social value of natural areas is not given its proper significance through a free market partly because many processes are
irreversible and partly because the preferences of, among others,
future generations and real devotees are not reflected well by it.
The 'revealed preferences' active in the market are in fact primarily bound up with present income and income distribution, whilst
income elasticity is difficult to measure. That is why a monetary
valuation of a real natural area is, in practice, so difficult.
It is easier, if the area in question is to be used for recreation.
We are mainly concerned here with emphasizing the significance of
the relative site, i. e. in relation to the residential centres, particularly the central agglomeration of a city district. However we
determine the price of land – by the market or through inquiries,
it is a function of, among other things, this relative site, because
of the costs in money and time accompanying the bridging of

distances. For this reason in particular, pressure will usually be exerted to convert land use in the areas close to the large centres. As far as the present situation is concerned, this conversion will involve agrarian land mainly with industry, housing, traffic, recreation and/or forms of subsidiary space occupation derived from these, as most important alternative uses.

The conservation problem in parts of Central Africa, for instance, is of course much less concerned with the tensions arising from a spatial structure characteristic of our environment. The necessity there as well, for conservation of 'wild parks' stems from the sharp rise in spatial mobility, resulting in a world-wide interrelationship expressed so accurately in Forrester and Meadows' model. It is therefore regrettable that this model is not spatially differentiated.

The problems concerned with the question of p o l l u t i o n are quite different. Here, the relation with the spatial structure is obvious. A notable feature is even that the pollution question can also be approached through an analysis of the (indirect) space occupation, as defined above. The essence of this theory can be formulated as follows:

1. the establishments for the various forms of economic activity are interrelated to such a degree, that a s p a t i a l a g g l o m e r - a t i o n in the form of cities, city districts, and urban zones, appears;
2. this spatial conglomeration increases the chance of (both positive and negative) e x t e r n a l e f f e c t s;
3. this manifests itself chiefly in an increase of s p a c e o c c u p a t i o n and the accompanying subjective experiencing of an increase of the pressure on the quality of life.

A practical distinction can be made here into:

a. e c o n o m i c external effects; and
b. p h y s i c a l nuisance effects.

The first can be described roughly as the effects which producers or consumers exert on other producers or consumers wholly or partly outside the market relations, which are not (or not fully), incorporated in the price mechanism and are therefore not (or not fully) compensated; the total social costs are therefore not (or not sufficiently) reflected in the price. As soon as the effects are (well) priced, they can no longer be seen as external effects, in the economic sense (Mishan, 1971), since they are then fully reflected in the price and there is no longer any incorrect allocation of production factors, from a social point of view. The foul smell and noise etc. still remaining can therefore, in an economic sense, be regarded as 'correct' pollution, belonging to a socially optimal allocation of production factors, with a given distribution of income. It should also be noted here that the pollution by consumers in this situation has not been properly calculated into the 'optimality' of the allocation.

The p h y s i c a l nuisance effects, priced or unpriced, remain, on the contrary, in the same form. (Economic) optimal pollution also, is still pollution. In practice, this can be expressed, for example, in the minimum norms which the government maintains in its environmental policy. These are norms which have not been made any lower so as not to cause any undesired results for other phenomena, such as, for example, employment.

A further problem is that with fully priced effects, no solution has been found for the problem of the nuisance itself. For example, an industry can produce, completely within the socially established norms and bear all the (relevant) costs while the remaining emission can still mean a considerable infringement on the well-being of a (probably very small) group of local residents. The relation offender-victim is then not direct, although the offender has indeed honoured the norms required by the government (public interests) or the required levy or retribution. This theory considers that the optimum has still been achieved with regard to the adoption of the Hicks-Kaldor criterion, whereby distribution is waived. Contrary to the original, Pareto criterion, considered to be unrealistic, this theory assumes that it is only relevant if the t o t a l compensation is sufficient to cover the t o t a l loss of prosperity, irrespective of who will receive the compensation. It is particularly important here, to use an approach from within the spatial structure, because this enables us to pinpoint the practical imperfections of the above criterion, since the people with lower incomes are often those who live there where the nuisance is most strongly felt: in the vicinity of industries and roadways and in obsolescent inner city districts. Mishan (1968) says that 'the poorer the family, the less opportunity it has to move from its present abode. On all counts, it is riveted to its domicile and must accept whichever impossible living conditions come its way. ' In other words: the poorer one is, the more enforced inconvenience one has to endure from the nuisance or the space occupation of others. To these and other conclusions, Mishan is also convinced of the need for so-called 'rights of live-ableness' and 'separate facilities'. We will be returning to this later on.

Firstly we will ascertain the degree to which the different forms of environmental pollution are related to the spatial structure; in turn, pollution of, or through, or by means of:

a. air;
b. water;
c. surface and solid waste;
d. noise.

ad a. air pollution

Various authors have already pointed out the following two phenomena, which are closely related to spatial structure:
1. The strong influence of d i s t a n c e on the concentration of polluting gases or solid particles (e. g. soot); diffusion models

assume by definition a decrease in concentration with an increase in distance (ceteris paribus);
2. synergism which refers to the combined effect of gases and solid substances, which is stronger than that of gases alone. Smog is a typical example of this.

In the first phenomenon, the distance between polluters and recipients is of vital importance. In the second it is the density of spatial concentration of polluters and the nature of the emission and the meteorological circumstances. It is also important to pay attention to the mobility of the polluters. Factories stay at a given place and motor cars move around. This fact is of course significant for the measuring and suppressing of air pollution. Finally, space occupation itself is also relevant, since it is very closely related to the possibility of influencing density.

ad b. water pollution

Contrary to air pollution, which, being dependent on the way the wind is blowing, can in principle go in all directions, water pollution is much more tied to the waterways, both natural and artificial, such as rivers, canals and drains.

The great rivers, such as the Rhine, because of their navigability and situation have had an important influence on the spatial concentration of economic activities. On the other hand, the larger urban areas have led to the construction of channels, canals, drains and also water purifying plants. The pollution of water is thus especially concentrated in places where the establishments of producers and consumers are concentrated, partly because above a certain degree of pollution, the self-cleansing properties decrease sharply. Serious forms of pollution can also appear near more isolated industries, such as strawboard factories and the bio-industry. A point to be observed is that water purifying plants often occupy a relatively large amount of space.

ad c. surface pollution and solid waste

This form is also closely connected with urban zones. The enormous piles of solid household and industrial waste constitute an important problem. What are we to do with it? To begin with, we have 4 possibilities:
1. incineration;
2. compost production;
3. re-cycling;
4. storage.

Because of relatively high transport costs and economies of scale, re-cycling is only really possible in large urban zones. Incineration occurs to an increasing degree per city district. In view of the shortage of raw materials, incineration is only justified if the paper

can be sorted out and the ash regarded as 'mine' from which the
minerals would have to be extracted, perhaps at the cost of a great
deal of energy. If this shortage is going to be very large in the
future, the storage of solid waste for a future generation with
greater technical knowledge is probably a good alternative. Both
the 'production' of solid waste as well as the economics of re-
cycling are coupled to large urban zones. In her book 'The Economy
of Cities', the American planologue, Jane Jacobs even speaks of the
cities as the mines of the future.

ad d. noise nuisance

The production of noise and the nuisance it causes are also often
coupled to larger population concentrations and modern technology
which does not aim at prevention of noise. Noise is, even more
than air pollution, sensitive to distance. An important difference is
however that noise ceases when the source of noise no longer exists,
while gases and waste substances continue to be present. Noise
nuisance is very closely related to the spatial structure. The system
of communications, the relative sites of homes, airports or beat
cellars etc. , are all dependent on the spatial structure of the economic activities for their location.

Finally we must emphasize that the different forms of pollution can
merge into each other. Incineration of solid waste can lead to air
pollution; water pollution produces solid waste (among other things
sewage sludge); prevention of air pollution in an industry can cause
an increase in the production of solid waste. In any case, practically all efforts to combat pollution use energy, which in turn has
to be produced from raw materials, which in turn have to be delivered, thus causing an increase in transport.

3. Environmental administration and physical
planning

The economist will at first be inclined to look for the solution to
environmental problems in intervention through the market mechanism, while the instrument of physical planning is intervention
through the data, or in other words the limitation or conditioning
of the free operation of the market mechanism. It is wise to pause
here and consider Mishan's belief (1968) that it is not the market
mechanism itself which has failed, but rather the legal framework within which it functions. He says further: 'we should, in
particular bear in mind that for a commercial enterprise, the
implication of the term "costs" is dependent on the law. If the law
allowed slavery, then labour costs would amount to no more than
what it costs to catch a man and then maintain him at the minimum
level of subsistence. '

The free market mechanism as such has been altered to such an extent by restrictions through laws and regulations etc., that the most effective means to influence market behaviour is no longer through price. This is even more so when decisions are involved that are determinant for the system and are applicable during a longer period. A choice situation of this kind is concerned with the determination of the future production and consumption structure, the kind of energy, the extent of the (de)centralization of the decisions etc. Intervention via the data will then be more effective. This does not imply however, that levies should not be used at this level since they do, in any case, have a signal effect and ensure that the government takes the (future) shortage seriously, strives after limitation and/or substitution and does not shun an adaptation of the system to achieve this. Intervention via prices is for simple choice situations, i.e. those at an executive decision level, certainly effective and mostly the cheapest instrument. Examples of this are the substitution of butter by margarine, of a soap containing phosphates by a soap not containing phosphates. In those cases - where comparable substitutes are available and there are sufficiently high demand elasticities - a price-raising tax is an excellent means of influencing the market. To influence the spatial structure, however, it will be necessary to intervene particularly via the data.

Mishan, however, recommends interventions mainly via the market and suggests two solutions to the problem of the 'preservation of the market':

1. to arrive at 'rights of livableness' via legislation; a conditioning of the market for external effects such as the right to sit in one's own garden without being hindered by the noise of the neighbours' electric lawn mower, unless the neighbour pays a sufficiently high compensation sum. In this way, those who cause the inconvenience are forced to bear the rise in costs. The external effects have been given a price and put on the market; and
2. the organisation of 'separate facilities'. Mishan means by this that separate areas are created which can be used by like-minded people. It is possible, for instance, to equip a beach for people who do not want to be annoyed by the blaring radio of a sunbather addicted to noise. The same applies to aeroplanes, which should only be allowed to fly over certain parts of the country and motor cars, which should be barred from certain streets.

The first proposal is quite inapplicable to compensation payments. Air pollution, for instance, has a pronounced and changing diffusion pattern, so that it is very difficult to point to the individual offender. This applies even more to the victims. The effects of pollution which is accompanied by unpleasant smells can be ascertained to some extent. But the long-term effects of non-smelling gases on health can be very serious, although this cannot exactly be measured. Compensation payment is then ridiculous, since it is not known who, where and what has to be compensated. The only remaining possibility is just to prohibit or regulate the emission, in which case there is nothing new or specific about Mishan's first proposal.

Our reaction to the second proposal is more positive although it is not a revolutionary new proposal either. In fact, p h y s i c a l p l a n n i n g in several countries (the Netherlands, e. g.) is based partly on that principle. The designation of industrial areas, the designation of natural reserves, even the division between residential and working areas, the banning of motorways from built-up areas etc. , are all examples which show that all that is new is the name. As early as 1923, this principle was laid down in the Charter of Athens, by town planners from many countries.

We can conclude, in general, that a radical change in the present spatial structure would take considerable time and absorb too large a part of the financial resources. This does not mean that no improvement can be achieved through physical planning. We must realize however that we have to proceed from the e x i s t i n g structure and that sizeable alterations at a macro level in the spatial structure take much time.

The spatial m a c r o - s t r u c t u r e (the national and international structure) cannot or can hardly be influenced within a short space of time, to say nothing of the question already mentioned above whether or not the government has the necessary power and resources.

The m e s o - s t r u c t u r e (the regional or city region structure) presents several possibilities. The location of the industrial areas, the motorways, the type of public transport, the laying out of parks and recreation areas etc. make it possible to counteract unpleasant effects. Causal factors such as emissions and the discharge of polluting substances, as well as the production of noise are not dealt with. The nuisance experienced by man is removed, moved or postponed; the damage to the natural environment continues.

The m i c r o - s c a l e presents, however, numerous possibilities to prevent or combat external effects - not without reason also called proximity effects! The planting of a green belt (see Maas and Beenhakker, 1969) between a factory or a motorway and a residential neighbourhood, the construction of residential districts free of motor cars, the avoidance of horizon-spoiling flats, the location of new residential and working areas alongside the rail infrastructure (see Lambooy, 1975), town renovation, the construction of a good sewage system etc. ; these are the activities which clearly show where the strength of regional planning lies: at the micro level. Although the increasing scale enlargement has demonstrated the disadvantages attached to this, the law has unfortunately not yet been adapted. This does not alter the fact that structurally, physical planning is extremely complicated on a meso and macro scale.

Our conclusion is that physical planning cannot be regarded as the primary means of solving the problem of the environment. It can, however, bring about the abovementioned improvements. It can also be used to protect natural areas (see Spoelstra, 1973 and Vellema and De Groot, 1971) but it virtually never removes c a u s e s, except in those cases where the problems are enclosed within the spatial structure itself, such as visual (horizon) pollution, suburbanization and congestion, obsolescent city centres etc.

The answer to the problem of environmental p o l l u t i o n will therefore have to be found primarily in changes in:

1. raw materials;
2. production processes;
3. products;
4. producer and consumer behaviour.

Except for the last category, the changes are primarily a question of technical development. They can be enforced by the government through prohibitions, levies, retributions and subsidies aimed at research and applications (see Lambooy, 1973). Another possible solution is of course the r e d u c t i o n of production and consumption.

In conclusion, we can say that economic activities, localized in 'establishments' as they are, are spatially interrelated to such an extent that it must be considered impossible to bring about any radical change in the spatial structure in order to suppress the external effects adequately. Intervention via the market by means of price increases does not produce enough of the results needed for dealing with environmental pollution. Other elements from the constellation of data will have to supply the principal means for solving the problem. The emphasis will have to be on the development and application of technical knowledge, the cultural pattern and the legal institutions, in particular. The fact that physical planning and intervention via the market can also provide an essential supplement, especially at the lower levels, is beyond dispute.

Notes

1. Capital-intensive industries are practically always industries which take up a lot of space, such as steel mills and refineries.
2. In my introduction to the National Conference of Economists in Rotterdam (1973), entitled 'Environmental control as allocation problem', I distinguished between the following levels (from high to low): 1. system determinant; 2. project bound; 3. executive. I would now like to combine 2 and 3 to make 3 and insert in the second place the i n s t i t u t i o n a l level to coincide with the classification found in an article by Ciriacy-Wantrup (1971), which has recently come to my notice.

References

Ciriacy-Wantrup, S. V. , 'The Economics of Environmental Policy', Land Economics, Febr. 1971, pp. 36-46.

Eucken, W. , Die Grundlagen der Nationalökonomie. Berlin-Heidelberg, 1965.

Lambooy, J. G. , Mensen en Milieu: op zoek naar een theorie, Tijdschrift voor Stedebouw en Volkshuisvesting, Aug. 1970, pp. 291-294.

Lambooy, J. G. , Leidse Baan: conflict tussen vervoer en milieu? Bouw, 1972, no. 1, pp. 13-16.

Lambooy, J. G. , Milieubeheer als allokatievraagstuk, Paper at the National Conference of Economists, Rotterdam, Febr. 1973.

Lambooy, J. G. , Economie en Ruimte. Van Gorcum, Assen, 1975.

Lerner, A. , On instrumental analysis. In: Heilbroner, R. L. (ed.), Economic Means and Social Ends. Prentice Hall, Englewood Cliffs, 1969.

Maas, F. M. , and A. J. Beenhakker, Groenzones en industrieterreinen, Econ. Stat. Ber. , 1969, pp. 148-153 and pp. 180-183.

Mishan, E. J. , The rights of man and the rape of his environment: a blueprint for a peaceful revolution, The Spectator, 14-7-1967, pp. 44-45; also Econ. Stat. Ber. , 20-3-1968, pp. 242-245.

Mishan, E. J. , The postwar literature on externalities, Journal of Economic Literature, 1971, pp. 1-28.

Spoelstra, M. , Ruimtelijke Ordening en de zorg voor het milieu, Tijdschrift voor Stedebouw en Volkshuisvesting, Febr. 1973, pp. 70-75.

Tihansky, D. P. , Economic models of industrial pollution control in regional planning, Environment and Planning, vol. 5, no. 3, 1973, pp. 339-357.

Vellema, K. and I. de Groot, Ruimtelijke ordening en natuurbeheer, Tijdschrift voor Stedebouw en Volkshuisvesting, May 1971, pp. 206-211.

Environmental and Region. An Orientation concerning Decision-making

A. J. Hendriks and J. Blokland

1. Introduction

Our aim in this chapter is to discuss a number of aspects which may, to a greater or lesser extent, play an important role in a situation where regional authorities are faced with the decision whether or not to permit the establishment of industrial activities in their region.

Obviously, before making a decision about industrial activities, it is essential to consider as many aspects as possible so that the final verdict could be described as 'carefully considered'. Since many industrial activities cause a considerable amount of air pollution, environmental aspects have to play an important part in this decision-making process.

Since the list of aspects to be discussed is no trifling one and our contribution here is fairly limited, it will have to be the multiplicity and variety of the relevant decision variables which engross the reader rather than the profoundness of our observations on these aspects. Four main categories of relevant aspects will be discussed in more detail. We have endeavoured to include labour market and economic aspects as well as sociological and environmental aspects. This analysis will not be presented here in an abstract framework. An attempt will be made to illustrate the analysis directly on the basis of a concrete regional planning problem. This concrete example concerns the possible location of an integrated iron and steel factory on the so-called Maasvlakte (the sand flats at the mouth of the Rhine, near Rotterdam). Before we proceed any further, it will be necessary, however, to describe in more detail the locational advantages of the Maasvlakte.

2. The significance of the Maasvlakte as an industrial site

The locational conditions required by an integrated iron and steel works become fairly obvious, if we study developments in the choice of location for this category of industry in general. The historical location (of industry) has always been the coal-mine area, but a number of factors have caused this to change to an increasing degree during the present century. These factors include: the change-over to other fuels, the rise of the scrap market, the integration within the iron and steel industry as well as the introduction of deep-lying iron-ore tankers and the expansion of the consumer market. We will be giving some attention to each of these aspects below.

Improvements in the blast-furnace technique itself led to the introduction of a different fuel mix. World War I led to an increasing substitution of coal by coke which meant a saving in transport cost. Coke has the added advantage of being porous and coke fires can therefore be fanned better. The injection of natural gas into the air stream resulted in an even more efficient use of heat. All this has caused the ties with coal areas to become looser.

The second factor is the rise of the scrap market. Increasingly greater consumption of iron and steel means at a later stage an increasingly larger supply of obsolete iron and steel constructions and thus of scrap-iron. Because of this increase in the supply of scrap and because of developments in technology resulting in greater possibilities for the recycling of iron and steel, the scrap market has become much more significant as input-factor.

Moreover, the processing of scrap uses less fuel than the processing of ore, which intensifies the tendency of scrap-processing blast-furnaces to be situated in the neighbourhood of their consumer markets: the fact that in countries with a pronounced industrial development, the scrap market and the sales market overlap each other geographically to a considerable extent is an important reason for the development of blast-furnace works in Japan and Italy, neither of which countries has any deposits of ore.

From this point of view, a location at the mouth of the Rhine, within the vicinity of the large consumer and scrap markets found in the 'Rimcity' of Holland, the Ruhr area and South-east England, is an interesting proposition for a steel works.

The third aspect is that of the integration of the iron and steel works, i.e. the inclusion of the production of pig-iron and raw steel is one production process.

A series of experiments succeeded in producing a high degree of so-called heat efficiency. The amount of fuel needed per ton of steel (originally much higher than for pig-iron) has now been reduced to approximately the level needed for a ton of pig-iron. The heat of the blast-furnace can thus be used for both the production of pig-iron, raw steel and plates, but this requires integration. Integration and concentration create scale benefits, which have been given a new dimension by the introduction of the deep-lying ship for the transport of ore. Ore tankers of 100,000 tons can enter only a limited number of ports and the demands made by such quantities on the transport overland are not inconsiderable. Large production units on the coast are ideal in such a situation and it is not surprising that with expanding consumer markets, iron and steel works tend to move to the coast in many countries.

Our conclusion is that from the point of view of managerial economics, the mouth of the Rhine does appear to be an extremely attractive site for a steel industry, for the following reasons:
a. it is then possible to use deep-lying ships to carry iron ore and fuels, while natural gas supplies would seem to be plentiful;
b. there are extensive scrap markets in the vicinity,
c. there is also a large consumer market for iron and steel.

3. Labour market aspects

In this section we will attempt to determine what the direct effects of the establishment of a steel-works could have been on the labour market. We will take a pragmatic view and not concern ourselves with the desirability of a specific development. We will, however, investigate what the consequences of the developments on the labour market would have been for the business cycle. We will deal firstly with the effects on the demand side.

Assuming full employment in the Rotterdam area before the construction of a steel-works, there are in principle, the following possibilities:
a. commuting;
b. migration;
c. immigration.
Obviously, the steel-works itself will make only limited use of these possibilities. Because of the level of skill that is required, it will have to appeal to the skilled labour already employed in established industries in the Rotterdam area. This appeal could be successful since the steel works are in a position to pay a lure-wage since the site on the Maasvlakte is very favourable from a private economic point of view. This means that the existing industries will then be compelled to grasp one of the three abovementioned possibilities. Since commuting has already assumed considerable proportions and since surrounding areas are developing rapidly at present, this possibility offers little solace. Large-scale migration into the Rotterdam area does not seem possible either since, in the first place, people in the Netherlands are reluctant to move and in the second place the tendency is, in actual fact, towards migration away from the Rotterdam area (see also ad 5).
Consequently, the only remaining possibility of any significance is the immigration of foreign labour. Our comments on commuting and migration are even more applicable here, i.e. the skill of the substitute labour will be lower than that of the workers who have gone over to the steel-works. This can weaken the competitive position of the existing industries.

In the foregoing, we have more or less assumed that a reallocation of the labour force can be achieved by means of a lure-wage. Is the formation of wages as simple as this, in reality? The fact that the realized wage rate increase exceeds the increase of the productivity of labour could lead to the conclusion that the average wage rate change is determined more by the development of productivity in the rapidly growing branches of industry than by the average growth. An increase in the wage rate in the Rotterdam area, induced by the steel works there, will certainly have repercussions on the wage front all over the Netherlands.

In short, when the supply of and demand for labour on the regional market are in equilibrium, the arrival of a steel-works would seem to push up the wage rate, not just in that region, but over the entire country. Because of the limited possibilities of a wage policy which is differentiated according to regions and branches of industry, both strong and weak industries encounter the consequences of an increase in the wage rate. This increase will, at least in part, have to be compensated by increases in prices, and the inflation spiral is thus completed.

Because of the level of the investments needed for a new steel-works of the required size and the time which elapses before the new concern is in full operation, enormous demands are made on the capital market. An additional inflatory impulse then follows.

4. Structural-economic aspects

We will now attempt to formulate some criteria which can be used to assess the long-term desirability of the establishment of a new integrated iron and steel complex. We will consider, first of all, how this complex stands in relation to the national objectives.

4.1. Economic growth

In order to trace the contribution of a steel-works to economic growth, we can make use of the concept 'growth potential'. The growth potential of a complex represents the direct increase of, for example, the number of filled labour positions or the net additional value.

As well as a direct increase, however, there will also be an indirect increase; namely that in other industries. Both effects together warrant the introduction of the concept 'cumulative effect'. The iron and steel industry is indeed a rapidly growing branch of industry, as Table 1 indicates.

A striking feature is that growth in the USA stagnates after 1965, while it continues in the USSR, to such an extent that about 1970-1971, the production in the USSR exceeds that of the USA. Japan too goes through a period of rapid growth - production more than doubled every 5 years. Japan climbed from an insignificant position in 1954 - still below BLEU - to the third position, where it even seems to be developing into a threat to the, up till recently, unassailable position of America. It appears that the relative growth

Table 1. Production of raw steel and pig-iron in millions of tons

	Raw steel				Pig-iron			
	54	60	65	70	54	60	65	70
USA	82	92	122	122	53	61	81	83
USSR	41	65	91	116	30	47	66	86
BRD	20	34	37	45	15	26	27	34
UK	19	25	27	28	12	16	18	18
Japan	8	22	41	93	5	12	28	68
France	11	17	20	24	9	14	16	19
Italy	4	8	13	17	1	3	6	8
BLEU	8	11	14	18	7	10	13	16
Netherlands	1	2	3	5	1	1	2	4
World[a]	224	330	446	579	155	228	311	410

a. Excluding the People's Republic of China.
Source: Yearbook 1972. Iron and Steel, Statistical Bureau of the EEC.

of the production of the EEC during the period 1954-1970 lags only slightly behind the relative growth of world production. This lag is, however, perceptible in the production of Great Britain. On the other hand, production growth in the Netherlands and Italy has been, relatively, the most rapid. Production in the Netherlands has been speeded up so much that at the end of the period, the production/consumption ratio was more than unity for the first time. This path of growth in time can be seen clearly in Table 2.

Table 2. Production and consumption of raw steel in the Netherlands in tons (× 1,000)

Year	Production	Consumption	$\dfrac{\text{Production}}{\text{Consumption}} \times 100$
1956	1,051	2,691	39
1959	1,678	2,740	61
1962	2,096	3,037	69
1965	3,145	3,823	82
1968	3,706	4,438	84
1971	5,083	5,078	100

Source: Yearbook 1972. Iron and Steel, Statistical Bureau of the EEC.

In the period 1959-1971, the production of pig-iron and raw steel was tripled, while the number of working hours rose by only 40%.

It seems likely that the development of the iron and steel industry has, in the past, been conducive to a greater diversity of economic activities in the Netherlands. As long as production and consumption differ greatly, the product in question is relatively undiversified. If production is attuned to consumption, we may ask if the optimum level of production has not been reached. If the production is relatively small in relation to consumption, the industry is not, or only slightly dependent on the business cycle. If, however, a further expansion of the production of raw steel and pig-iron is pursued, then this expansion will be concentrated on export in particular and can, partly for this reason, lead to a greater cyclical susceptibility.

The establishment of basic industries without the associated iron processing industries has the additional drawback that although the Netherlands has to bear the environmental costs (to be discussed below) the benefits, in the form of income-producing activities higher up in the business column (in casu the activities of the steel processing industry which are much less detrimental to the environment) are reaped abroad, in West Germany, among other places.

In other words: only a limited part of the cumulative effect of a new iron and steel complex on the Maasvlakte is realized within the Netherlands. From a national point of view, this implies a reduction of the growth potential of this concern.

4.2. Full employment

If our goal is long-term full employment then we must aim at as little unemployment as possible and as few vacant positions as possible. Demand and supply will, therefore, have to be attuned to each other. Training and stimulation of mobility among other things can exercise an influence on the supply side of the labour market while stimulating and restraining measures present certain possibilities on the demand side. The plan for a new steel-works would have to be evaluated in the light of the desired structural development of both the national and regional labour markets. Because not much is known about the subject, we can only suppose that the introduction of a steel-works will not result in any particular consolidation of the structural equilibrium on the labour market.

4.3. Other national objectives

Stabilization of prices, distribution of income and equilibrium on the balance of payments are objectives yet to be discussed. Stabilization of prices has in fact already been discussed in Section 3. The distribution of income will be treated in 4.5, while we touched on the balance of payments in 4.1 and will not be discussing it any further.

72

4.4. Regional economic growth and employment

Some of the regional economic objectives are derived from national objectives such as economic growth and employment while some of them have a specific character, e.g. the regional distribution of income. Finally, some of the national policy objectives play hardly any role regionally, e.g. stabilization of prices and equilibrium on balance of payments.

The economic growth in a region must be attuned to the situation on the labour market. Development of a branch of industry which is fairly new for a certain area must be in accordance with the expected development on the labour market. If a structural increase in the supply of skilled labour is to be expected then an attempt must be made to adapt policy to this. Prolonged economic growth cannot be realized in a monostructure where a region is, in fact, supported by one 'strong' branch of industry. This is because in the course of time, every branch of industry undergoes a certain development: rise, stabilization, stagnation, decline. A great variety of different industries, in many different phases of development, can be an important guarantee for structural prosperity.
This leads therefore to the conclusion that the Rotterdam area must not be completely dependent on oil for its well-being but needs a second pillar as well: a steel industry. This would cause diversification to increase and would guarantee a greater potential prosperity. The first question which arises is whether both pillars are sufficiently independent of each other. They are both industrial pillars while a pillar in the services sector would perhaps be preferable. Developments in the supply side of the labour market point in this direction. It is probable that expansion of economic activities which have adverse effects on the environment would not obstruct this more preferable development.

4.5. Regional distribution of income

When regions register different long-term rates of economic growth, there will be an increasingly greater difference in prosperity between the regions. This can result in a relative decline in prosperity. Because no-one is in favour of such a development, an attempt will be made to distribute the wealth more or less evenly over the nation. This means stimulating measures for backward regions and restraining measures for the regions with the most vigorous growth. In this way, an effort is made to bring about a balanced spatial distribution of economic growth.
It seems unlikely that a steel industry on the Maasvlakte would contribute much towards the desired equilibrium. From a structural point of view, we may expect to find the seat of the overheating of the Dutch economy in the Rotterdam area. If there is any need for a steel-works in the Netherlands, and this is doubtful, there would

in any case seem to be many risks attached to the Maasvlakte as a possible site.

4. 6. Flexibility

By the flexibility of an existing regional economic structure towards a specific new complex, we mean the ease with which such a complex is integrated. This flexibility is therefore inversely proportional to the resistance towards incorporation of the new complex in the existing regional structure. Some of the factors which affect this flexibility are:
1. the presence of the required number of skilled labourers;
2. the sociological situation in the region;
3. the present infrastructure, insofar as it is relevant to the complex in question;
4. the present degree of air pollution and water pollution and the emissions of the complex.

It is not easy to overestimate the importance of this flexibility. Incorporation in an existing economic complex despite opposition can lead to the expulsion of other parts of the economic structure ('bad industries drive out good industries'). An unwelcome industry can cause the outflow of high-grade concerns and highly skilled workers. It seems that the present pressure on the environment does indeed lead in the Rotterdam area to an outflow of concerns and employees. We will return briefly to this when we are dealing with environmental aspects. Firstly, however, we will consider the sociological situation in the region.

5. Sociological aspects

In Section 3, we saw that in the Rotterdam area there are in fact three possible means of obtaining the extra workers necessary for setting up a steel-works: commuting, migration and immigration. We will now consider the sociological aspects of these possible solutions. At the request of the OECD, L. H. Klaassen and P. Drewe (1973) have made a study of migration in several of the member countries, i. e. France, Great Britain, the Netherlands and Sweden. They attempted to explain the interregional migration streams by means of three factors:
- the size of the non-agrarian employment in the area of destination;
- the total professional population in the area of origin;
- the distance between areas of origin and destination.

The above authors came up with the following results for the Netherlands:
1. By far the smallest reaction in the volume of migration arising from the supply of labour positions in the area of destination

74

(France displayed a relatively large reaction, while Great
Britain and Sweden shared a position in between).
2. A large distance-sensitiveness (this was slight in Sweden, while
France and Great Britain were in between).

We may conclude from this that the relative lack of willingness to
migrate has not only been an impediment to the development of the
northern part of the Netherlands but could also obstruct ambitious
plans in the south-west of the country. In the 1950's, when there
was a relatively large amount of unemployment in the northern
areas and a shortage of workers in the Rotterdam area, a migration
policy aimed at stimulating the transfer of workers was introduced.
This policy was not particularly successful; neither were efforts to
transfer central government departments. Migration is apparently
something which cannot be forced.
The most important incentive for commuting (at least with regard to
long-distance commuting) is income, but one is forced to accept
longer travelling time and less leisure, in return. This can have
repercussions on a harmonious family life and a healthy social life.
Any enthusiasm for doing something worthwhile in one's leisure
time, could very well be destroyed by the extra fatigue of travelling.
The preference of income to leisure can therefore be temporary.
This brings us to objections from the entrepreneurial world. Will
the phenomenon of commuting be permanent or will it eventually
disappear? Is it a firm enough basis for an investment policy? In
view of its aims, regarding regional policy and regional planning,
the government can decide that the phenomenon of commuting does
not solve regional labour market problems and can prefer to adjust
living and working in each separate region. This has the added
advantage that the burden on the infrastructure is reduced to a
minimum.
In the past, slavery was a method of getting cheap labour to do work
which was unattractive to free citizens. The reason for this could
be that the work was physically exhausting or particularly unpleasant or that the prestige attached to the work was negative.
Immigration of foreign workers bears some resemblance to a
modern form of slavery and certainly does not function as a means
of improving onerous working conditions. Without these possibilities
of immigration, our society would have to seek other solutions:
mechanization, automation, rises in status, higher pay, lightening
of too heavy labour etc. Immigration of foreign workers does tend
therefore to preserve social ills in one's own country and does not
present any solution for the labour market problems in the foreign
worker's own country. It is therefore neither a development policy
for one's own country nor one for the country of origin. Foreign
labour can be justified only if the training a foreign worker receives
will enable him to occupy a useful position in the production process,
upon his return home.
Actually, a policy favouring the immigration of foreign workers
seems to conflict with the avowed preference for a zero population

growth. Another facet of the question of foreign labour is accommodation. These workers are in fact forced to look for accommodation in the older areas, with low rents. This is one of the causes of the minority problem which has arisen in some residential quarters of Rotterdam. This phenomenon can cause considerable social difficulties.

6. Environmental aspects

When investigating the effect on the environment of a steel industry, we find on the one hand consequences which are relatively simple to quantify, such as the emissions but on the other hand, consequences which are less easy to quantify, such as the decrease in the attractiveness of the immediate environment.
The report of the Governmental Commission on Protection of Surface, Water and Air (1970) contained the following figures concerning the emissions in the final phase of the construction process of the Hoogovens concern, with a production of ten million tons of raw steel per year. Emissions per day:
- sulphur dioxide   55 tons;
- nitric oxides   45 tons;
- particulate matter emission 75 tons;
- fluor   6 tons;
- carbon monoxide   800 tons.
Excluding the steel-works therefore, approximately 600 tons of sulphur dioxide is emitted per day in the whole Rotterdam area. This means that there will be a considerable absolute increase of pollution, although it is in fact a relative increase of only 8% more sulphur dioxide. In addition, the steel production involves the emission of:
- metal oxides;
- sulphur hydrates;
- tar drops.
There will also be some water pollution.

Even if we disregard the size of these figures, we can conclude that there will be a deterioration in the appreciation of the immediate environment, in the relations between man and his spatial surroundings. It is important to keep in mind that space is not an abstract category, but is expressed by means of a concrete structure. This spatial structure includes at least three elements: nature, capital and man himself, individually and as a group. By nature, we mean air, light, water, greenery, etc. Capital is found in many different forms; invested in buildings, streets, squares etc. The social environment, manifested in the presence of individuals and groups can also be interpreted as a part of the spatial structure.
Degradation of a spatial structure can occur through a decrease in the quality of each of these elements separately as well as combined.

Careless maintenance can be the cause of degradation of the element
of capital. The arrival of population groups with different customs
and ways of life can signify a deterioration in the minds of the
original inhabitants of a residential quarter. However, pollution
of natural elements such as air and water is also degradation. We
can then say that the degree of deterioration in one element can in
concrete cases be compensated by improvement in other elements.
The ultimate total effect then depends on balancing the two.
A distinction can also be made between absolute and relative degradation. Relative degradation can occur even in the absence of absolute degradation of a spatial structure through information about
new, more attractive spatial structures elsewhere. This too can
cause changes in the appreciation of a concrete regional spatial
structure.
The regeneration of a degraded regional spatial structure to a
higher level of appreciation is a collective matter. In such a reconstruction area, all kinds of special public provisions and reconstruction activities are applicable.
Reactions to a degradation are conceivable at an individual level as
well. These reactions could be said to depend on the size of the
costs involved in avoiding a spatial structure considered to be in-
convenient, the level of the income and the willingness to add these
avoidance costs to one's budget. This willingness should be regarded as a separate factor, since activities in the field of communication,
such as education, press, radio and television do have a certain
influence.
We can conclude therefore that a continuing increase in prosperity,
as well as an extension of education, guidance and other forms of
information are all stimulating a manner of behaviour containing an
increasing opposition to environmental pollution and also an increasing
avoidance of the consequences of this by migration abroad. It is
reasonable to assume that those with the best training will then be the
first to go.

7. Conclusion

Probably the best way to summarize the foregoing would be to proceed from two possible situations involving the Rotterdam area.
Alternative A presents a situation with a new steel complex on the
Maasvlakte and alternative B a situation without.
As we have shown above, alternative A illustrates the enrichment
of the Rotterdam area with a healthy and vital industry. Employment
opportunities expand, diversification in basic economic activities
increases, and national economic growth receives a vigorous
impulse.
On the other hand, this alternative is not without a number of
problems. Existing industries experience difficulties because of
an exodus of personnel. Inflation is stimulated. The immigration
of foreign labourers increases. We can expect an increasing number of

high grade companies and highly skilled personnel to move away. More pressure is put on the environment. In short: the Rotterdam area is on the way to becoming a second Ruhr area - with all its merits and demerits.

If alternative B is chosen, then these drawbacks are avoided but a policy aimed at the revaluation of the spatial environment and its component parts then becomes necessary. This policy should also aim at stimulating a greater diversification of economic activity particularly in the tertiary and quaternary sectors of the regional economy. We should have made it clear now that, in our opinion, it would be incorrect simply to reject the plan for a steel complex on the Maasvlakte. Rejection should be accompanied by a well-considered suggestion for an alternative possibility and an appropriate well-formulated and well-prepared policy. There can be no question of missed chances then.

References

Drewe, P. , B. van der Knaap, G. Mik and H. Rodgers, Segregatie in Rotterdam. Netherlands Economic Institute and Economic-Geographic Institute, Rotterdam, 1972.

Eijk, C. J. van, 'De Nederlandse Economie van 1973', ESB, 28 Oct. 1970.

Governmental Commission on Protection of Surface, Water and Air, Report. Rotterdam, 1970.

Isard, W. , 'Some locational factors in the iron and steel industry since the early nineteenth century', The Journal of Political Economy, 1948, p. 203.

Klaassen, L. H. , and P. Drewe, Migration Policy in Europe. A Comparative Study. Saxon House, Farnborough, 1973.

Ronteltap, R. , and J. Funken, Ruimteconsumptie of bouwconsumptie? Kluwer, Deventer, 1972.

Roscam Abbing, P. J. , Ethiek van de inkomensverdeling. Kluwer, Deventer, 1973.

Some Implications of the Costs of Environmental Policy

G. F. A. de Jong

1. Introduction

Not so very long ago - in the fifties, in fact - smoking factory chimneys were the symbol of employment and therefore of prosperity. The more chimneys there were, the more work and prosperity there was.
This does of course still apply. No, or at least not enough, attention was paid however, to the reverse side of the picture: the harmful external effects of not only the growing industrial concentrations but also the clusters of people living together in a confined space; the use of new substances which are difficult to destroy and the rapid motorization and disfigurement of the countryside by asphalting.
In the sixties, however, the realization that there was an environmental problem grew rapidly. Surface, water and air were and still are being polluted in a way which we cannot accept. The recognition of the problem resulted in the hasty formulation of an environmental policy, based on a constantly expanding legislation. The measures, both past and future, issuing from this legislation will obviously affect the enterprise, especially the industrial enterprise.

2. Public policy and private enterprise

Environmental measures influence the enterprise in three different ways: they drive up costs, they limit freedom and increase uncertainty. This sounds rather negative but no criticism is implied in this trio.
That environmental measures drive up costs will be obvious to everyone, even without further explanation. We will however be referring to this aspect later on.
By the limitation of freedom we mean that radical demands are imposed on the establishment of enterprises, on the issue of a permit to allow the enterprise to continue operating in the same place, on production methods and the use of land, auxiliary materials and energy etc.
The increased uncertainty issues from the fact that the enterprise

does not know, or does not know precisely enough, which environmental demands will be made on it in the future, which criteria will
then be applicable, the rate at which the demands will have to be
satisfied, the costs which will be involved etc.

The three points mentioned above make it essential that enterprises
are able to get used to the new legislation. This means they will
have to be informed early on, of the details of the intended environmental legislation, of the criteria which will be maintained, the
actual moment of introduction and any temporary measures. They
will therefore desire talks with the government and a say in framing
the rules which are going to apply to them. These talks and the
participation can be broached by an individual enterprise but also
by a group of enterprises; via a regional organization, their branch
organization or their central organization.

These talks are not only important to the enterprises but also to the
government, so that the government is aware of the consequences
of intended measures for the enterprises. Without discussion,
without preliminary information about the policy to be pursued, the
trio - rise in costs, limitation of freedom, growing uncertainty -
can have such a negative effect on the business climate that this
can suffer unexpected and unintended damage.

3. Cost estimates

How large, in money terms, is the problem of the environment in
the industrialized countries? Although no exact figures are available,
we do have estimates which do not vary as much now as they did
several years ago.

In January 1972, the Federation of Netherlands Industry (VNO) estimated
ƒ 4-5 milliard per year for the overtaking of arrears and the elimination and prevention of environmental pollution in the Netherlands.
This figure is made up as follows: cost of overtaking arrears ƒ 0.5
milliard; cost of extra investments needed to ensure that new machinery is clean in operation ƒ 0.25 milliard; cost of changing the
production processes and raw and auxiliary materials ƒ 0.75
milliard; personnel costs ƒ 0.5 milliard; levies, claims for
damages, etc. ƒ 0.1 milliard: or a total of ƒ 2 milliard. Assuming
that the costs borne by industry for a clean environment amount to
about half of the total annual cost of preventing or counteracting
environmental pollution, the total annual costs will amount to approximately ƒ 4-5 milliard. (1)

The estimate in the same year by the Ministry of Economic Affairs
in 1972 was 2% of the Gross National Product (GNP) as additional
increase in costs for overtaking existing arrears. If this increase
in costs were to be realized via a regular annual increase (somewhat more than 0.5% of the GNP) up to about 1975, then this would
take up more than 10% of the annual growth estimated for the GNP
for following years. The extent of the stabilization of the percentage
share which could then appear, would depend in the first place on

new technological developments, of which re-cycling processes can play an important role.
The OECD has also published a number of estimates from different countries (Analysis of costs of pollution control, Paris, 1973).
Some examples are: USA 2.2% GNP (yearly average 1971-1980); West Germany 1.8% GNP (1971-1975); Italy 0.6% (1971-1975); Japan 2.2% (1971-1975, investments only). The OECD draws the following conclusions from these figures which cannot be compared to each other:
- the costs of combating environmental pollution are considerably lower than a number of other categories concerned with public welfare (public health, education);
- environmental measures lead to a shift in the allocation of the national income but not to one that is larger than many, earlier shifts;
- the costs of environmental control will probably increase in all industrialized countries, although to a varying extent, as a result of differences in population density. This international increase mitigates the effects of the costs of environmental control on the international balance of trade and balance of payments.
Our reasons for paying so much attention to the estimates concerning the costs of environmental control are twofold:
1. substantial sums of money are concerned, approximately half of which will be chargeable to industry, assuming that the estimated extent of the pollution by industries and the costs of elimination and prevention of pollution are in proportion;
2. the various estimates show how much uncertainty there still is about the cost of a clean environment, even more uncertainty if we consider that these estimates do not include any definition of how clean a clean environment is.

4. Public opinion and sacrifices

Not only is the enterprise confronted by an increase in costs through prevention or removal of environmental pollution, it is also faced with restrictions arising from environmental policy, as we have already indicated above. These restrictions can concern establishment requirements but also the promotion or prohibition of certain production processes or of certain products. We also acquire, on the other hand, new productions, such as of cleaning machinery etc. In short: shifts in the production pattern and the growth pattern will appear, which the government will deliberately encourage.
Such a development is not an essentially new element for an enterprise if and inasmuch as it merely anticipates expected developments; developments which will be strongly influenced by a switch in public opinion about the dangers which are threatening the environment. Only a decade ago, the only ones to be alarmed by the advancing environmental decay were a few nature lovers and biologists etc. In 1970, an investigation carried out by the Netherlands

Central Office of Statistics showed that more than half of the Dutch population believes that environmental pollution can lead to a catastrophe involving the very existence of humanity.

The continuous and unsolved public discussion on growth, employment and environment corroborates what we have so far been able to ascertain with regard to the distribution of the growth in prosperity. The community constantly has to decide where to allocate the economic growth: environment, housing, education etc. or more to private purses. The outcome of the yearly battle concerning the assignation of the growth does not make us optimistic about the willingness to make sacrifices for the environment.

A real willingness will mean that on the 'means side' the enterprise must be capable of enduring the financial consequences arising from environmental measures without endangering its competitive position or long-term profit.

On the 'expenditure side' however, the growth of real consumption from private and government sectors will have to decrease as a result of passing on the environmental costs to the individual consumer or to the whole community. This entails deliberate investment in 'unproductive' capacity, since environmental investments alone do not contribute directly to enlarging production. The value we attach to our life climate is expressed by these sacrifices.

May the enterprise expect this development and anticipate it in its policy? Unfortunately, past experiences show that we can expect that the enterprise will be expected to make sacrifices which should in fact be borne by the whole community. In other words: the enterprise is treated as if it is the only source of pollution. It is common knowledge that there are several other polluters - households, traffic - which are together responsible for half to two-thirds of the pollution.

There are therefore uncertainties about the size of the environmental costs and also uncertainties about the distribution of the costs involved in cleaning up the environment and keeping it clean. There is, finally, uncertainty about the significance and execution of the principle 'the polluter pays'.

5. The principle 'the polluter pays'

What does the polluter pay exactly, or what should he pay? For a discussion of the subject that not all costs are included in the price of a product and that unpriced negative external effects appear, which require correction by governmental measures, we refer the reader to a wide variety of recent publications. Here, we only wish to point out that there are still many unsolved problems concerning the way in which this unpriced scarcity should, in practice be determined.

It is a well-known fact that in many countries legislation proceeds from the principle 'the polluter pays', to which we would like to add: 'according to the extent of the pollution it causes'. The polluter pays

in order to prevent undesired environmental effects or to eliminate
them. The principle does not therefore constitute an excuse to continue (at a price) polluting. The enterprise itself can take measures
to prevent or eliminate environmental pollution (as other polluters
can do) or it can, by payment of the costs (levies), for which environmental facilities have been and are being provided by the
government, use these collectively available facilities (e. g. water
purification plants, incinerators for solid and/or liquid waste material etc.).

6. The levy and the principle 'the polluter pays'

The principle 'the polluter pays' is still far from definite. This is
not surprising since this 'principle' originally meant only that the
costs of combating and preventing environmental pollution should
not be charged to general resources of the government.
The legislator (at least in the Netherlands) has definitely not had
and still does not have a clear vision of what these costs are composed of and which criteria should be used to charge them to 'the'
polluters. Despite this, environmental levies have been firmly
anchored in the environmental legislation right from the beginning.
At the moment, the levy (being an attractive means of contributing
to the government till, even if it is not used for environmental
purposes) is rapidly gaining ground.
We have already seen above that the principle 'the polluter pays'
cannot be interpreted merely as the imposition of levies. A considerable proportion of prevention and elimination of pollution by
(industrial) concerns occurs within the concern itself, in particular
of course the pollution which has to be suppressed at its source.
The levy will only begin to play a part in legislation if the government assigns itself a role in combating environmental pollution
(construction of purification plants) or has an advisory function
(eliminating the effects of environmental pollution by compensation
paid from a funds created by levies).
Certainly where industry is concerned, the principle 'the polluter
pays' can chiefly be realized without any levy at all (purification of
water in own installations, dust particles removing plants, re-
cycling systems, noise suppressing provisions). Permits required by law regulate which provisions a concern should have in
order to prevent environmental pollution beyond the limit which is
tolerated. (We will return to these limits of tolerance later on.)
Up to this point, the principle is clear and not too difficult to put
into practice. The difficulties arise however, when the polluter
does not take the counter measures himself, i. e. as soon as the
government takes measures collectively and charges the costs to
all those who pollute albeit in different ways and to various degrees.
Which costs can be allocated to polluters and which criteria must be
maintained so that not all polluters will be treated alike but will each pay
according to the extent they are responsible for the pollution and the

measures taken against it. This sets limits to the application of levies. The use of the levy is correct if it is aimed directly at covering the costs incurred by the government for the prevention, elimination or limitation of environmental pollution (retribution). Such measures can, in principle, be taken by industry itself. An optimal approach can require however that the measures are taken collectively. The authorities - a municipality or a drainage or purification district - acts in such cases as a service-rendering authority for population and industry and can thus demand a price which covers the costs. The costs of inspecting if the environmental laws are being obeyed and of controlling the development of the environmental situation (e. g. costs of the necessary official apparatus, the erection and maintenance of measuring networks, emission registration etc.) are not classified as the rendering of services to polluters since the authorities do not incur these costs for the sake of the polluters alone but in their function as guardian of the public interest. If there were any retribution here, then this should be paid by the whole population equally and not only by industry and that part of the population which could be regarded as polluters, as in fact occurs at present.

A situation of c o m p e n s a t o r y levies is somewhat different. The proceeds of these levies are given as compensation to polluters who, as a result of the government's environmental policy, find themselves faced with costs which they should reasonably not, or not in full, have to continue to pay. The proceeds can also be given as compensation to those who suffer from the air pollution e. g. by damage to crops or stock. We are concerned in particular with those cases where no private legal settlement is possible (for instance, when the identity of the offender is unknown).

In our present legislation, physical regulations are the appropriate policy instruments for achieving certain environmental hygienic objectives. However important the levies themselves may be, their only function in this case is to provide the government with the financial means needed to help realize these objectives. Only in the case of compensatory levies is this somewhat different.

7. Theory and practice

It seems so perfect: the levy both as a means of suppressing what is tabu from the point of view of environmental hygiene (prohibitive levy) and as a means of adding the unpriced harmful environmental effects to the (too low) market price.

In practice, a large number of objections adhere to this theory.

In the first place, social costs cannot be determined because, for one thing, we know too little about the harmful effects on the environment of criticized production techniques and products and their substitutes. One may not expect any optimal allocation either, since the levy will, in practice, be only a more or less successful approximation of the social (environmental) costs which have not yet been allocated. This pessimism is not however complete: the chance of making important mistakes with this 'pricing' has not yet been discounted. We must take good note of energy-devouring or polluting re-cycling processes and of doubtful substitutes, e. g. replacement of phosphates by NTA. In such cases, there is no question of improved allocation.

In the second place, a realization of what the theory advocates is impeded by monopolistic positions, irreplaceability of products, meagre demand elasticity of products and price ratios already confused by excise duties.

For example, by reducing some of his profit per product - perhaps even by an amount equal to the fixed levy, an entrepreneur can still be competitive. If he relinquishes even more profit, then, with a large demand elasticity, his turnover in the unclean product may even increase, producing effects incompatible with the aim of the levy.

It is also possible that cost price components of the unclean product decline, which would be reflected in the price of the product and its sales. The levy would therefore continually have to be manipulated. Since, moreover, specific levies finance the collective environmental facilities, the government would have the proceeds of the prohibitive and allocative levies at its disposal to 'spend at will'. It is conceivable that a lengthy continuation of substantial environmental pollution is in the government's interest.

To return to our starting point: the levies we have just mentioned would confront enterprises with completely unfounded higher costs and even more uncertainties. If and in so far as regulation is considered necessary, there are other, more efficient instruments available (prohibitions, rationing, injunctions etc.).

8. Environmental costs: production costs

For the enterprise, the costs of prevention or elimination of environmental pollution are production costs. Like all costs, environmental costs will be passed on into the prices of goods and services. They are charged to the consumer ... at least if the development of demand and supply factors permits.

Environmental costs for the same product often differ however; according to producer and place.

These differences depend on the site of an industry, the degree to which the site is already polluted, the limit of tolerance at that spot, the legal regulations concerning environmental hygiene. They exist on a national and international level and have an effect on and sometimes even determine, the competitive position.

It is a well-known fact that frequently environmental costs differ widely per region. Significant differences in levies for discharging waste water indicate that the gradualness of the introduction of purification works in various parts of the country has been ignored, although there need be no objection to regional differences as such in the size of the levy.

We do advocate however more uniformity in the levy policy, especially with regard to the rate of development of the environmental policy, the norms to be set up, the calculation methods and the methods of depreciating and obtaining money etc.

In view of (international) competition it will often be impossible to pass on the costs of environment improvement wholly or even partly into the final price.

Temporary government assistance (e. g. the compensatory levy already mentioned which is used to assist enterprises which have to carry higher environmental costs than can reasonably be expected of them), government subsidies and fiscal facilities can play a role here. If these are unavailable or insufficient, then the environmental costs will be charged to the profits, as long as there is sufficient profit.

With regard to government assistance, we must bear in mind that subsidies or payments from funds with the sole aim of preventing the transmission of environmental costs into consumer prices, will inevitably lead to the same artificialities as do exist in housing and agricultural policy.

Financing out of profits will definitely not be possible for low profit branches of industry.

9. Costs: a matter for the whole community

Our point here is that the expense of a clean environment is not only a problem for enterprises, but is also a problem which directly concerns the whole community.

If we find that the costs of a clean environment threaten the continuity of industries or even of a branch of industry, then there are two possibilities: either to discontinue the industry in question or provide financial help with environmental costs because, for example, the employment it provides is vital to a certain area.

The same involvement as that of the community in the problem of the environmental costs of enterprises appears if one refuses to accept harmful effects which arise from the international competitive positions of enterprises, which have been altered by environmental costs.

The position is no different when enterprises have insufficient possibilities or willingness to make investments since their profit development will decline when environmental costs are drawn from the profits.

The involvement of the community is also expressed in a different way. We have already used the term limit of tolerance several times. Two limits can be distinguished:
- the limit of pollution, transgression of which will threaten life itself;
- the limit determined by what people in general are prepared to accept, socially. This limit of tolerance is determined by existing local or regional demands with regard to improvement of the immediate environment.

With increasing prosperity, the limit shifts towards even less acceptance of pollution. Increased prosperity also enables people to place more exacting demands on their immediate environment. This implies at the same time that the enterprise must reckon with increasingly exacting environmental requirements and therefore with increasingly higher environmental costs.

The limit of tolerance is determinant for the extent of the suppression of existing pollution. It is therefore essential that growth of prosperity in the traditional sense and desires with regard to a clean living climate be attuned to each other.

It is the task of the government to determine where the limit of tolerance will lie at a given moment and then develop the norms needed to effect the suppression of environmental pollution to the limit of tolerance.

10. Fiscal concessions

A possibility would be the introduction of an investment deduction for investments in the environment and/or accelerated depreciation. Examples of the various forms which facilities can assume can be found in other countries. The Swedish government, for instance, has since 1969 been giving industrial enterprises subsidies of 25% of the costs of environmental investments. This subsidy has not, however, had much effect. In December 1971, the subsidy percentage was raised to 75% (partly in order to stimulate the business cycle).

In other countries, concessions are of a more fiscal nature. In the USA, the costs of installations for the prevention or limitation of pollution can be written off in 5 years, if the costs are incurred for factories which were operating before 1st January, 1969.

In West Germany, 50% of the initial or production costs of movable installations (which includes all factory installations) and 30% of immovable installations can be written off earlier. Here too, this facility applies only for measures in existing factories.

In France, various facilities are provided among which an accelerated depreciation in the first year of 50% for immovable constructions aimed at decreasing pollution of air and water.

In England, accelerated depreciations for such installations are no longer necessary. Industrial enterprises are now allowed to write off their investments in machines and installations for 40% in the very first year. In addition, investment subsidies of 20-22% are granted to industries in development areas in England.

The objection which can be raised to facilities such as accelerated depreciation for environmental investment is that it is difficult to find a criterion to differentiate the proportion represented by environmental investments in the total investments. This difficulty has apparently been overcome abroad by the appointment of an impartial body which decides which part of the investments of an enterprise can be regarded as having been made in order to prevent or eliminate environmental pollution. A body of this type can be found, for example, in West Germany and USA.

A good environmental legislation, implying a consistent application of the principle 'the polluter pays' as well as a transmission of environmental costs into the price of products (and where this is not possible due to competitive situations, the introduction of fiscal facilities) will make it possible to cleanse the environment and keep it clean within the prevailing system of free enterprise.

Note

1. The annual costs estimated by the Central Planning Bureau in 1975 amount to f 4. 5 milliard.

Environment and Economic System

F. Hartog

1. Delimitation

The private enterprise system can be blamed for the present environmental problem since it nurtures individualistic calculation methods and individualistic business activity. Only one's own costs and benefits are taken into consideration and negative repercussions of production and consumption on others are ignored.

The next logical step would be to suggest that our present system should be abandoned and replaced by another system with many more governmental decisions on economic matters, since the government is obliged to consider all repercussions.

There is a risk that by pursuing this line of thought we make light of two considerations which can plead for certain relativity.

In the first place, it is quite conceivable that the problem in question can be solved or in any case nearly solved within our own system. In his observations on the means of economic policy, Tinbergen distinguishes quantitative means, qualitative means and reforms. (1) Among quantitative means (or instruments) he includes changes in quantity, such as tax rates, rate of discount, rate of exchange etc. within a given economic structure. Qualitative means alter the structure itself within given foundations, e. g. the introduction of a new tax or a new social insurance. Changes in the foundations themselves are what he calls reforms. What is involved here is the transformation of the economic system, for example by nationalization of private enterprises.

It is reasonable to assume and also fairly generally accepted that if the government has a choice between means with a fairly equal degree of effectiveness, it should always use the least drastic. This is because the more drastic the means, the greater, in general, the resistance to the adjustment and the habituation and by frequent use of drastic means the greater the uncertainty in society.

We must, therefore, always look for quantitative means first, then qualitative means and only then transformation of the economic system.

This is the first plea for relativity. For our purpose, the task then follows of investigating to what extent the environmental problem can be solved at all adequately within our own system.

There is, however, a second point. Assume that we do indeed have to turn to reforms because we have had no or not enough success with quantitative and qualitative means. Must we then discard our system? Since only half of the proof has been provided we cannot say this for sure. We would first have to have evidence that there is at least one other system which can indeed handle this problem. It must, moreover, be a system which can function in reality. It would be no use designing a Utopia peopled by individuals who exist wholly for the community. That would be unrealistic.

The concrete alternative which we will examine is a system with exclusively or predominantly public enterprise and the majority of the population, like people all over the world will be neither completely good nor completely bad.

It is not our intention to adopt an empirical procedure and use a numerical comparison to choose the system which is most friendly to the environment. However attractive this may seem at first glance, it is not necessarily conclusive. This is because other variables such as the degree of economic development and the population density are involved in such a comparison. This can cause a systematic distortion, in so far as countries with a system of private enterprise are, in general, the countries with the highest degree of development. In so far as the degree of environmental pollution is positively correlated with the degree of economic development (which can reasonably be assumed), it would seem obvious that the problem of the environment appears first and, up till now, foremost, in the private enterprise system. It is possible that the other systems have not or not yet reached this stage. We suffice here with noting that environmental pollution appears under all existing systems and that in our system, public enterprises are also responsible.

In other words: the problem of the environment could very well be non-system-bound. In itself, it constitutes a technical phenomenon (in a broader sense). What is important is the extent to which an adequate solution is possible within different systems. For this purpose, we will have to take recourse to a deductive reasoning, but with a view to reality.

The foregoing represents a certain delimitation of our problem. In the following we will firstly substantiate the simplification which we make of the classification of the economic systems.

2. The two alternatives

The contrast with which we will be concerned is therefore that between production by private enterprises and production decisions made by the government. This closely resembles the more politically charged contrast between capitalism and communism. The two contrasts can indeed be broadly identified with each other, but not before making some nominal refinements. Capitalism and communism both have what we could

call respectively a m a r k e t v a r i a n t and a s t a t e v a r i a n t. The market variant of private enterprise could also be called m a r k e t c a p i t a l i s m. Opposed to this we have s t a t e c a p i t a l i s m, which is a system we find in many developing countries. The state acts as most important producer but without the ideological basis of communism. On the other hand, communism contains as market variant, the system of labour management, on which Yugoslavian communism is substantially based. The other communist countries could be called s t a t e c o m m u n i s t. (2)
We are particularly concerned here with market variants on the one hand and state variants on the other hand. Of the market variants, the capitalist is by far the most important and of the state variants, the communist. We would not be very wrong therefore if we simply spoke of the contrast capitalism-communism. We could perhaps also call it individualism versus collectivism. Individualistic systems are aimed essentially at the maximization of profit (in the capitalist variant) or of labour income (in the communist variant). In both cases, this implies a certain stylization but otherwise these systems are not, or hardly, suitable for a generalizing analysis. As we have said, we hope here to arrive at general insights, with reality as our inspiration but not aiming at an exact replica of it. (3) Consideration of external effects does not in itself fit in with such a maximization unless based on governmental measures. This last point brings us to the question whether or not market systems (we have selected private enterprise as the most important representative) are compatible with effective suppression of environmental deterioration. We will be concerned with this problem in detail below.
On the other hand we may also, for our purpose, identify state capitalism and state communism with each other. Both are concerned with production decisions (in the broadest sense) which are taken by or on behalf of the collectivity, with the government operating as executive body of the collectivity. Where such a collectivist system exists, whatever its ideological basis may be, there is in principle a direct possibility to take environmental factors into consideration. This also forms the basis for the previously propounded belief that collectivism is better for effective control of environmental decay than individualism. It remains to be seen if we continue in this belief after we have gone deeper into the matter. The difference between maximization of the income of one of the participants by operating on the market at one's own risk on the one hand and production decisions (in the broadest sense) made by government bodies on the other hand can also be described as the difference between the p r i c e m e c h a n i s m and the b u d g e t m e c h a n i s m. We must, however, keep in mind that functional government bodies can, to a certain extent, be authorized to use their own income for their own expenditure, without having to ask permission every time. Ultimately, public enterprise remains something which is always governed by budgetary rules so that the distinction 'price mechanism - budget mechanism' can indeed be used.

Can we identify the contrast in question with the distinction 'de-centralization - centralization'? No, we cannot, since the government can also act in a decentralized form, both in a territorial and functional sense. As we will see, it is precisely this point which is of great importance in the assessment of the effectivity of collectivist systems in suppressing environmental decay.

Is it still necessary to pay extra attention to indications we can get from occasional public enterprise within an otherwise individualistic system? An illustration from real life: in the Netherlands, many municipal councils have replaced clean trams by dirty buses (4) and a subsidiary enterprise of the state mines discharges poison into the river Rhine. It does not therefore seem to make any difference whether private or public enterprise is responsible for production. It is not as simple as this however. For reasons of competition public enterprises often have to follow the market and therefore the behaviour of private enterprises. On the other hand, public enterprises often occupy a monopolistic position in their branch of industry. The monopolistic character of, in particular, public utilities was originally one of the reasons for government exploitation. Since there is then no direct competition there will be at least some opportunity to take environmental factors into consideration. Another possibility would be to grant a subsidy to public enterprises which do take environmental factors into account when making their decisions, corresponding to the extra costs they thus incur, so that if competition did arise they would be capable of standing up to their private colleagues. This brings us back to our subheading of the instruments of government policy, which we will discuss further below. We are left therefore, with mixed feelings towards the activities of public enterprises within a system that functions, as a whole, individualistically.

A certain tardiness, too, would seem to be evident which can also apply to environmental decay under collectivist systems, especially where there are industrial concentrations. The problem of the environment has not been the focus of attention for long and the government, acting as producer also needs some time to become aware of the problem and adapt its decision standards. This is an additional reason for not regarding the available, empirical data as conclusive and preferring to attempt to penetrate beneath the surface of things.

3. Environmental problems in individualistic systems (5)

In private enterprise, environmental damage appears, in general, in the form of negative external effects of production and/or consumption. These are the harmful effects experienced directly by others through the production and/or consumption, without any compensation being paid by the offender. His calculation of costs does not therefore include the negative external effect. This causes costs to be too low, in the sense that they do not reflect the complete scarcity of production factors. As a result of this, the price at which the relevant products will be delivered will in general also be too low and will lead in turn to a more than optimal consumption. In short, the problem of the negative external effects can be incorporated into the theory of welfare economics. This is the branch of economic science which concerns itself with the conditions under which welfare is maximized. (6)

Because of this, the question which concerns us can be formulated thus: which economic system is most able to realize the optimum conditions of welfare economics on this point?

One of the first economists to be specifically concerned with the relation between negative external effects and economic system is Tinbergen. He regarded it as a part of his investigation into the optimal economic system. (7) He investigated in particular which factors can cause a divergence between individual decisions and optimal welfare: if this occurs, then he recommends that the production be taken over by the government.

He classifies external effects (both positive and negative) among these factors. For him, therefore, they constitute a decisive reason for nationalization. (8)

It is strange that Tinbergen does not follow the comprehensive view on the means of economic policy which we have mentioned beforehand. When there are external production effects, the alternative he recommends is either private or public enterprise. If the latter occurs in considerable proportions then it amounts in fact to a choice between two different systems. He thinks, therefore, more in terms of reforms than of qualitative or quantitative means. This is even one of the elements of his so-called convergence theory which deals with establishing closer relations between private enterprise and state communism. (9)

Typically collective goods such as 'safety' and 'order' (10) appear foremost among the examples he gives. For this reason we believe that Tinbergen is referring here only to production processes with very important external effects. Collective goods can indeed be regarded as an extreme case of (positive) external effects. It is a borderline case, because there is no longer any private activity which summons the external effect as (undesired) side-effect: the external effect itself is the aim of the production of the good in question by the government. In other words: the good and its external effect co-incide here.

In any case, in those instances, e. g. with regard to environmental pollution, where the external effect is indeed an undesired by-product of activities which are themselves aimed at other things, it is wise to ask ourselves if qualitative and especially quantitative means also exist to reconciliate private decisions with optimal welfare.

If we then follow the theory of welfare economics, we can say that the divergence between individual activities and optimal welfare can be imputed to the fact that there is no price mechanism for the relevant external effects. If they had a price which would have to be paid by the offender then the price mechanism would no longer work incorrectly and can therefore, in this respect, be relied upon as a guideline for making individual economic decisions. In terms of welfare economics, we call this the internalization of an external effect. If it concerns, for example, industrial emissions of dirt and/or stench in the air, or the din of aeroplanes, then this could be brought within the discipline of the determination of prices by presenting air as a production factor which we must pay to use. (11) The consumers of the goods which make use of this production factor would then be faced with the entire costs, also with those which apply to the negative external effect now internalized. Assuming that there are no other divergence factors, they will then reduce their consumption so far that the last consumed unit will exactly counterbalance its costs. This is another way of saying that (with a given distribution of income) the welfare optimum has then been reached. This will always lead to a reduction of pollution but not necessarily to its complete elimination. Even pollution becomes optimal in the sense that it only takes place when the disutility it causes is less than the utility attributed to the relevant internalized production factor.

Internalization of negative external effects can thus occur in various ways. It would perhaps be best to discuss this in a sequence which is related to the degree in which we move away from the system of private enterprise.

We are closest to the individualistic system when those who suffer inconvenience attempt to induce the polluter, by offering him money, to stop his emissions completely or partly (redemption). The polluter will in general be interested in such a transaction if and in so far as the loss of profit and the extra costs which accompany the limitation of the polluting emission are less than the sum which is offered to him. All this occurs via a voluntary market transaction. The determination of prices is perfected by this to such an extent that (excluding other divergences) optimal welfare is achieved. If we limit ourselves, for simplicity's sake, to the situation where the emitter has, as deciding factor, a reduction of profit, then this process of price determination can be reproduced schematically in a graph which is based on a corresponding representation in an article by Mishan. (12) The diagram can be found on page xx.

This figure illustrates the noise produced by an airport. The numbers of flights are set out on the horizontal axis, the profit of the airways and the compensation which the people living nearby are willing to pay, both per flight, are set out on the vertical axis. The curve ZSM represents the profit per flight. The curve OST represents the nuisance per flight, expressed as the maximum price which the neighbouring residents are willing to pay to be rid of the nuisance. Both curves are m a r g i n a l in that the profit and the sum which the residents are prepared to pay, if need be, are considered for each additional flight.

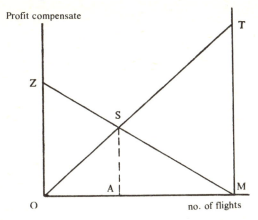

If the neighbouring residents do not initiate any action but merely grit their teeth and allow the nuisance to continue, then the airway companies, assuming that they aim at maximum profit, will continue their flights until point M has been reached. This is, however, clearly not the point where welfare is optimal. The profit can be regarded as the difference between what the passengers are prepared to pay for travelling by air and what it costs the airway companies (excluding the noise nuisance). It is therefore an index of the positive difference between the produced utility and the sacrificed utility (excluding noise nuisance). Past point S however, the noise nuisance expressed in money exceeds the profit as indicator of positive utility difference. In other words: the flights past S supply a positive utility for passengers, indicated by area ASM but for the neighbouring residents, they supply a negative utility as indicated by the area ASTM. Finally, the negative utility of the flights past S is represented by the area STM.

The optimal point is S where the marginal noise nuisance is equal to the marginal profit. To the left of this point, there is also less than optimum welfare because there the profit is greater than the noise nuisance.

If the neighbouring residents enter into negotiations with the airways, then the optimum will automatically be realized, since proceeding from point M they can, for every flight omitted, offer a sum which is larger than the loss of profit by the airways. This continues until both are equal, i. e. until point S has been reached. It is not a simple matter to estimate the size of the total money-sum which finally passes hands. It depends on the bargaining power of both parties. The neighbouring residents are prepared to pay a maximum sum of ASTM; the airlines want to receive at least ASM. The equilibrium sum will be somewhere in between. This has no effect however on the attainment of point S since the gap at the margin between what the parties want to pay or receive has disappeared. Only the intra-marginal sums which are paid cannot (within the above limits) be determined by using this analysis. This produces, however, an extremely idealized picture. If we apply the method of decreasing idealization and thus come closer to the complications of reality, we find that it is the friction in particular which causes this process not to run so smoothly as we have suggested above. There are, for instance, the transaction costs for the neighbouring residents which have to be subtracted from the benefit they can gain through negotiations. They will have to take counsel with each other and negotiate with the opposing party, resorting even to legal action. At this point we can for the first time bring the government into the picture since the government can assume payment of transaction costs and provide facilities for the negotiating process. Actually, providing the total transaction costs are lower than the minimum gain from negotiations, they do not necessarily lead to another optimum point as final point, since they form constant costs and do not therefore disturb the marginal curves: because the optimum point is determined by these marginal curves only, the transaction costs do not cause it to shift. These can, however, as we have said, be prohibitive.

With the appearance of the government as catalyst, we have therefore taken a step towards using certain means of economic policy to achieve the optimum.

Continuing along these lines, it is also conceivable that not those who are affected adversely by the nuisance should pay but those who cause it. This is a question of distribution policy, whose normative aspects fall outside the sphere of welfare economics. This does not, however, cause the optimum point to move and if the government has access to the same information as the victims, then it can also be reached by means of a levy on the polluter. The levy would then have to increase per flight along the curve OST. The government acts, therefore, to a certain extent, on behalf of the residents but a completely different distribution then arises. In this case it is best for us to start from point O. Up till point S it will be in the interest of the airlines to pay the levy because the profit exceeds the levy up to that point. Past that point, the reverse is true, so that S again becomes the point of equilibrium. The distribution of income then becomes completely different, as we see when a study of the various areas reveals who receives the benefits in both cases. So as not to make things too easy for ourselves we will also assume that in the case of spontaneous negotiations, the residents are able to extract as much as possible so that they can persuade the airlines to accept redemption money amounting to ASM. If there is a levy, they will not have to pay this sum, while the flights will still be reduced to the same point. If the government were to pass on the levy, involving an amount of OSA, to them as a compensation for the inconvenience they continue to suffer by the continuance of the number of flights OA, they would even r e c e i v e a sum of money instead of having to pay one. The size of that sum would be equal to what they would be prepared to pay to prevent the remaining flights as well.

We must repeat, however, that this has no influence on the position of the optimum and the attainment of the optimum, assuming that the government adjusts the levy to the costs of the noise nuisance, as expressed in the maximum buying off sums which the neighbouring residents are willing to pay.

With a levy of this nature, we depart somewhat from the pure market situation characteristic of an individualistic economic system. This is however also a form of internalization of external effects. Governmental action ensures that individual economic decisions are made to correspond with optimum welfare. In the whole market, the levy produces an additional factor that is carried into prices by means of an increase in the cost of production of goods with negative external effects. The fact that in this case the polluter pays does not therefore mean that he does indeed carry the burden. The levy is passed on into prices and over the heads of the producers, the consumers are hit by the higher price. They therefore limit consumption to the point where marginal costs, including marginal pollution, are equal to the price, the latter as an indication of the marginal utility (excluding other influences which disturb the optimum).

If a levy takes the disutility of pollution into consideration it does not impair the determination of prices but perfects it instead. Although the prices were distorted at first, they have now ceased to be so.

An anti-pollution levy can also have an effect on producer behaviour. If, for instance, we are dealing with a production process where pollution can be prevented by incurring additional costs, then the levy can be a stimulus to purify the production process in order to evade payment.

It is also possible that collective purification, e. g. sewage purification, would be more sensible. The government is then the obvious authority for carrying out the purification but it can pass on the costs involved to the polluters. It is also possible to make purification compulsory. The costs of the product and therefore its price would then increase automatically.

Which method is most suitable will depend mainly on the production process. What this all boils down in practice however, is that the price of the product increases with the purification costs, so that it is a correct representation of the costs incurred during production.

This is all based on the assumption that it is indeed technically possible to avoid the pollution or limit it. If it is technically possible, then there are no economic reasons for refraining from doing so, i. e. private enterprise is, in principle, capable of absorbing an effective anti-pollution policy without destroying itself. (13) It is even more likely that this system will be perfected further in this way. The determination of market prices, which forms its heart, is in case of external effects, to a certain extent distorted in that prices are not a completely accurate guideline for decisions. If external effects which culminate in environmental pollution are

interned in the determination of prices, then this is more able to fulfil
its function as a coordinating mechanism for economic action. In a way,
we can say that the deterioration of the environment is not the fault of our
economic system but of the inconsistent application of this system.
Another misunderstanding closely allied with this is the view that
to include environmental considerations in production and consumption decisions is the same as adding non-economic factors to
the purely economic weighing of decisions which has been practised
up till now.
Considered in the light of our previous line of thought this is exactly
the other way around. In short, economics is concerned with efficient
decision making. If incorrect calculations are made because environmental factors are not sufficiently taken into account, we can
say that not too many economic factors have been considered but too
few. Conversely, the introduction of environmental considerations
means that the activity becomes more, instead of less, economic. (14)
When purification is technically impossible (e. g. where irreplaceable natural scenery is threatened with destruction) and the wish to
stop or limit the activities is present anyhow, the only conceivable
solution is to prohibit the activities.
If it would be very difficult to carry out an effective control
of compulsory purification, it would then seem logical to think in
terms of a take-over by the government of the production involved.
If this occurs on a large scale, it becomes a reform à la Tinbergen,
and we find we have thus arrived in another economic system. This
is what happens in the extreme if we assume that the least drastic
means are always sought.
We should note here that the problem whether or not to stop or limit
economic growth (i. e. the increase in production) with regard to the
problem of the incorporation of environmental considerations in the
efforts to obtain optimal prosperity, constitutes a derived problem.
In other words: if enough attention is paid in economic policy, to the
deterioration of the environment, then we will automatically solve
the problem of economic growth. Production can be left alone if it
is based on correct signals. In fact, the transmission of the costs
of environmental levies will automatically have a negative effect
on the relevant activities, so that the composition of the growth will
change to such an extent that pollution will be reduced to the level
which corresponds to the desires of the economic subjects. Environmental policy is growth policy, or if one prefers, anti-growth
policy.

4. Environmental problems in collectivist systems

If we no longer know how to solve the environmental problems within
our own system, we can introduce an element from another system,
i. e. public enterprise. As we have seen, this can occur in particular
when we work with regulations for private enterprises which cannot; or only with difficulty be controlled.

Can, however, the budget mechanism (in a broad sense) achieve what the price mechanism cannot? We will now turn our attention to this question.

Firstly, let us put a strict interpretation on the working of the budget mechanism by examining the situation where a government body is subjected by authorizations for all expenditure either from higher bodies or by legislation.

Money is received for executing specified tasks as accurately as possible. At the same time, an account of how the money was spent must also be rendered. An enforced thrift replaces the discipline of the market: one must try to manage on as few financial means as possible or try to achieve as much as possible with a given amount of money. The emphasis is not on maximization of profit, but minimization of costs.

We, however, are concerned with the production of goods and services with negative external effects and then in such a way that the activities connected with it are all subjected to budgetary authorizations. A municipal council which absorbs a production process directly into its administrative activities, without giving it the form of an enterprise is an example of this. Can we treat environmental considerations in this way? Although it is, in principle, possible, the required administration does present problems. There could, for instance, be a decrease in the size of production or an increase in costs. Quantity clashes with quality (in general) and that, together with the thrift which public bodies should aim at (and do in fact practise, all being well), renders that environmental considerations can still encounter difficulties from government bodies. Working to an authorizing budget is a rigid approach, as a rule, and qualitative factors (which can include the suppression of environmental deterioration) can often be neglected in the process.

This is even more pronounced if we are concerned with a system that is based totally on public enterprise.

In such a system it is necessary that the whole production process be directed according to a plan and the separate enterprises be incorporated in the plan by setting standards. In other words: while the planning is necessarily centralized, executing it is necessarily decentralized. For this reason, it is incorrect, generally speaking, to identify a system with public enterprise with centralization, in contrast to market systems which would then have a decentralized production process. Production cannot in general occur otherwise than in a decentralized way. In systems with public enterprise, only the planning is centralized.

This brings us to state communism, in particular the Russian economy, which has the most experience with this system.

It appears to be unavoidable that the incorporation of the separate enterprises in the plan is, in such a system, practically a purely quantitative affair. The Russian economy is a quantity oriented economy and it appears to be not possible, or extremely difficult to allow qualitative considerations to participate in production decisions. (15)

The reforms which have been carried out since 1965 on the incorporation of production decisions in the plan have had virtually no effect. The number of quantitative norms is somewhat decreased and more attention is paid to the profit criterion (16) but it remains a matter of quantitative planning and execution. Only the use of sales instead of production as a norm can improve the quality somewhat but that does not help us to protect the environment. Furthermore, the advance of the profit criterion means only that in this respect there is a slight convergence to the system of private enterprise where, as we have seen, the pursuit of profit in itself clashes with the idea of environmental protection.

The reform of the economic system in Russia does not therefore point towards a better assimilation of environmental considerations. The fact that the environmental problem as such still plays only a minor part in the changeover to simplified production norms is not decisively important. It can be a question of backwardness, on the one hand because the level of prosperity is not as high as in the Western industrial countries and Japan and on the other hand because the realization of the problem takes time. (17) Of great importance, however, is that the whole system is little suited to include the quality of the environment among its planning standards. Inclusion of the suppression of environmental deterioration within the determination of prices by the market is not possible here, since there is no determination of prices by the market in production activities. A system with public enterprise is therefore more likely to lag behind a system with determination of prices via the market. There is however another aspect on which the two systems differ, or at least can differ. A system with predominantly public enterprise does not necessarily have to be guided by the wishes of private consumers in its production decisions (in the broadest sense). The government can wholly or partially make its own decisions regarding goods it will produce and in which quantities. A paternal attitude of this kind towards the consumers can manifest itself in two ways. If the consumers of certain goods are pressed into buying more of these goods than they themselves want, then we usually call these 'merit goods'. The degree to which the consumers can be forced on this point is of course limited: what they really do not want, they do not buy. There is no limit to the reverse, however: the goods which the government does not want the consumers to use ('demerit goods') are simply not produced in a system with public enterprise, or in smaller amounts than the consumers want. If goods with negative external effects were now to be labelled 'demerit goods' either in the production or consumption stage, or in both, then the external effects could be radically suppressed. In all probability, this would not result in a situation of optimal welfare but this is not the intention of a paternalistic government. Van den Doel, who has made a critical study of Tinbergen's convergence theory, emphasizes this point in his discussion of Russian consumer policy. (18) The attitude of the Russian government towards what it considers 'demerit goods' is not however motivated so much by environmental considerations as by ideological motives. Whenever there is a choice between individual and more or less collective consumption, the collective form will always be preferred. This is possible under the prevailing system simply by producing the relevant collective provisions but none or hardly any of the individual goods which aim at satisfying the same needs. Taxis are therefore preferred to private cars, laundrettes to individual washing machines, restaurants to private refrigerators, flats to one-family houses. (19)

This is what does actually happen but it could also be interpreted as suppression of environmental deterioration by classifying goods with negative effects as 'demerit goods' and stopping the production of such goods on these grounds. This does already happen to a certain extent but more by accident (discouragement of private car ownership for instance).

Precisely because the standard of living is not as high in Russia as in the western countries, it is still possible to prevent all kinds of developments which can no longer be undone in the west. The advantage of being backward is that one is able to take the lead all at once by putting the latest ideas into practice. However, this too has its limits. We have already called attention to the failure to pursue optimal welfare in the sense of adjusting the production as much as possible to the wishes of the consumers. In a way, this is not necessary either, because the government has its own preferences but it is not wise to depart too much from what the consumers want because of the tensions this may cause.

In particular, it may be expected that the more the production potential increases, the more difficult it will be to maintain the idea of underproduction of 'demerit goods'. In order to maintain full employment for all production factors, many more goods would have to be produced which the consumers would rather not have. As the standard of living rises, the consumer will become more particular and the risk of unmarketable surpluses will arise more often. That is the only way in which consumers in a paternalistic system can, to some extent, influence production decisions.

If our assumptions are correct, this possibility will increase as a more consumer-directed society develops in these particular countries. The possibility which exists, particularly in Russia, for applying the 'demerit' system for the suppression of environmental deterioration will then decrease.

An additional factor is that the very radical solution of stopping or almost stopping the production of goods with external effects is useful if the external effects are limited to a few instances but not if they are distributed throughout the whole production and/or consumption process. After all, it is not possible to stop or slow down production on all fronts. Only a few especially spectacular cases can be caught in this way. If negative effects (in many fields) are to be combated then it is still more effective to include the environmental considerations in the market mechanism - if it exists.

The third point, once again especially applicable to Russia, is the ideological attitude of the government in its production decisions. The environment does sometimes benefit from this, as in the opposition to private car ownership, but it can also lose, e. g. when at certain points prestige projects with important negative external effects are being pushed through (Tupolews!). This is not of course necessarily a general impediment in systems with public enterprise.

There is yet another characteristic distinction between an individualist and a collectivist system with regard to the suppression of environmental deterioration; one which is unfavourable to collectivism. It concerns in particular the distinction between individual and collective ownership of the material production factors.

We have already seen that an external effect can be checked by internalization, i. e. by subjecting it to the price mechanism. The whole trouble arises because air and water are free production factors, so that nobody has to pay for using them. Nobody, therefore, is presented with the costs of using them.

Originally, land too was partly common property. Therefore, no one had to pay a price, which would reflect the scarcity, for using it. This led in many cases to over-grazing. This is what, in effect, occurs with regard to air and water. (20)

Seen in this light, the collective ownership of land in collectivist systems is detrimental to the quality of the environment. No one has to face the depreciation of the land arising through wasteful exploitation, exhaustive cultivation and erosion. A private owner on the other hand must always try to keep up the value of his land in case he will want to sell eventually. This prevents some of the environmental decay which would arise under collective ownership. (21) Once we have determined the price (of environmental decay), all other things will follow.

Thus we conclude these digressions on the problem of the environment in a public enterprise system. They leave us with mixed feelings.

If we were to have the colours black, white and grey at our disposal, with white being an effective suppression of environmental deterioration, black the absence of suppression and grey (from light to dark) all that lies in-between, then we could describe the system of private enterprise as light-grey and the system of public enterprise as dark-grey with some patches of white. Do not however expect us to indicate the exact proportions!

Notes

1. J. Tinbergen, Economic Policy: Principles and Design. North Holland Publishing Company, Amsterdam, 1956, pp. 4/5.
2. For more details see F. Hartog, Economische stelsels. Wolters-Noordhoff, Groningen, 1970.
3. For the economic operation of the system of labour management,

with regard to the aim of maximization of labour income, see:
J. Vanek, The General Theory of Labor-Managed Market
Economies. Cornell University Press, Ithaca and London,
1970.

4. J. Pen, 'Zeven methoden van anti-vervuilingsbeleid: een poging
   tot systematiek', Economisch Kwartaaloverzicht Amrobank,
   March 1971.
5. See also M. Glagow (ed.), Umweltgefährdung und Gesellschafts-
   system, particularly part III, Umwelt und Kapitalismus. R.
   Piper & Co., Munich, 1972.
6. For a more detailed account, see F. Hartog, Toegepaste wel-
   vaartseconomie. H. E. Stenfert Kroese, Leyden, 1973.
7. J. Tinbergen, 'The Theory of the Optimum Regime', Selected
   Papers, North Holland Publishing Company, Amsterdam, 1959.
8. See Tinbergen, op. cit., p. 285.
9. He has devoted several publications to this, e. g. J. Tinbergen,
   'Do Communist and Free Economies Show a Converging Pattern?',
   Soviet Studies, April 1961.
10. See Tinbergen, op. cit., p. 293.
11. See particularly E. J. Mishan, 'The Postwar Literature on
    Externalities', Journal of Economic Literature, March 1971,
    p. 3.
12. Mishan, op. cit., p. 20.
13. A closely allied argumentation is to be found in J. Zijlstra,
    'Milieu en Economische Orde' in Tussentijds Bestek, Stichting
    Maatschappij en Onderneming, The Hague, 1973.
14. Hueting in particular has repeatedly pointed out this. See e. g.
    R. Hueting, 'De nieuwe schaarste is keihard', Economisch-
    Statistische Berichten, 1 April 1970.
15. There are numerous publications on this, e. g. various publi-
    cations by the English economist A. Nove. In the Dutch language,
    there are several fairly recent studies which provide extensively
    documented information: W. J. van der Molen, Economische
    hervormingen in de Sowjet-Unie 1965-1969; Universitaire Pers
    Rotterdam, 1970; and S. van Popta, Inhalen en voorbijstreven;
    Universitaire Pers Rotterdam, 1971.
16. Van Popta, op. cit., pp. 83/84 and Van der Molen, op. cit.
    p. 365.
17. For environmental pollution in Russia: M. I. Goldman, 'Um-
    weltzerstörung und Umweltvergiftung in der Sowjet-Union', in
    the volume by Glagow, already mentioned above.
18. J. van den Doel, Konvergentie en evolutie. Van Gorcum &
    Comp., Assen 1971, pp. 92-94 and 163-166.
19. Idem, p. 93.
20. See G. Tullock, Private Wants, Public Means. Basic Books
    Inc., New York and London, 1970, p. 149 et seq.
21. This point is mentioned by Goldman in particular, in the above-
    mentioned volume by Glagow, pp. 89/90.

Mondial Aspects of Environmental Problems

P. H. J. J. Terhal

1. Introduction

One of the objections to the report to the Club of Rome, mentioned
by Aurelio Peccei and Manfred Siebker in a paper written at the end
of 1972, is: 'LIMITS predicts hell in 50 years. Hell is already
present on earth in places such as Calcutta'. Peccei and Siebker
offer no further comment on this reaction. (1)
More official terms are used in the following quotation, taken from
the so-called Founex report on development and environment which
was compiled by a number of experts at the request of the Secretary
General of the United Nations:

'However, the major environmental problems of developing countries
are essentially of a different kind. They are predominantly problems
that reflect the poverty and the very lack of development of their
societies. They are problems, in other words, of both rural and
urban poverty. In both the towns and in the countryside, not merely
the "quality of life", but life itself is endangered by poor water,
housing, sanitation and nutrition, by sickness and disease and by
natural disasters. These are problems, no less than those of industrial pollution, that clamour for attention in the context of the
concern with human environment. They are problems which affect
the greater mass of mankind. '(2)

In the words of Barbara Ward:

'The natural resource most threatened with pollution, most exposed
to degradation, most liable to irreversible damage is not this or
that species, not this or that plant or biome or habitat, not even the
free airs or the great oceans. It is man himself. '(3)

The international aspects of environmental problems can no longer
be treated as a number of national problems with some external
effects on other nations. Less than 5 years ago, when the idea of
the Environmental Conference in Stockholm was first born, it was
expected that the conference would be concerned with local environmental deterioration appearing especially in the urban areas of the

highly industrialized countries and in the common problem of pollution of water and air. The appearance of the report to the Club of Rome, the participation of the developing countries in the conference and especially the participation of many ordinary people in the discussion have raised problems of a much more fundamental nature. One of these is whether and if so, under which social, political, cultural and economic conditions our fragile earthly ecosystem can offer a decent existence to an explosively growing world population.
This question is directly related to the matter of distribution: now that about 20-30% of mankind accounts for 80% or more of the total consumption of raw materials, it is very obvious where the most radical changes are needed. (4)
The extension of the concept 'environment' during recent years is partly due to the science of ecology. (5) This science emphasizes the fact that man is completely dependent on the earthly environment. (6) G. Picht says, rightly:

'The ecological crisis is thus not just a marginal phenomenon of our society. Environment is not just a setting; we ourselves are part of that environment. Just as an ants nest or a pack of animals, human society is a sub-system w i t h i n nature. We will only begin to understand human ecology when we realize that our economics, our politics, and even our science are activities within nature. How we change nature depends on how we act socially. '(7)

The social activities of man have, therefore, always been accompanied by changes in nature. This human interference can be summed up in 5 categories:

a. Agriculture and cattle farming
In order to satisfy his basic needs, especially for food, man (originally a hunter, fisherman and collector of fruit), changed over to systematic agriculture and cattle farming about 10,000 years ago, an occupation which has, in a short time, radically altered the appearance of the earthly environment.

b. Exhaustion of natural resources
In order to satisfy a number of largely artificially cultivated and acquired needs, man is exhausting, at an increasingly rapid rate, the supplies of certain mineral resources and fossil fuels.

c. Urbanization
In order to satisfy the need for concentration of activities, both industrial and cultural, huge urban agglomerations have arisen, in which the natural environment has been replaced by a completely artificial environment.

d. Pollution
In order to have an (apparently) cheap solution to the problem of the non-usable waste products often harmful to man and of side

106

effects of industry, agriculture, transport and consumption, waste products are just dumped in the earthly environment, in so far as they do not escape the control of man completely and side effects on nature are simply tolerated.

e. Destruction of the environment
In order to make certain regions of the world unfit for human habitation, extensive environmental destruction programmes have been carried out. For instance, 12% of the total area of South Vietnam has been sprayed with leaf-stripping chemicals and millions of bombs have been dropped. Similar things have occurred in Angola. The long-term effects of these activities on the vulnerable tropical soil will probably be very serious. (8)

Of course these five points do not pretend to be a complete list. Recreation and tourism, for example, deserve a separate mention. The most striking feature is that all these human activities do not occur independently but are bound up with each other and together form one large system in which the one element presupposes the other. Barbara Ward calls this system the technosphere. (9) Historically, this technosphere is rooted in the biosphere and the geosphere but during the last century, it has been developing more and more in a parasitic fashion, at the expense of the biosphere and the geosphere. The international or rather mondial aspects attached to the search for a new balance between technosphere, biosphere and geosphere are described below. In the choice of these problem areas, we have aimed at as wide an approach as possible.

2. Some economic consequences of the environmental crisis in the technosphere

The environmental crisis will have profound consequences for the international economic relationships between the highly industrialized countries on the one hand and the whole range of half-industrialized to least developed countries on the other hand.

1. Paradoxically, the economic value of certain raw materials can decrease as the rich countries, under pressure of imminent scarcity, will find possibilities for recycling, substitution or economizing. The solution of this shortage problem can in the long run very probably undermine the economic position of a number of developing countries exporting raw materials, although they can temporarily and in some cases, profit from a relatively comfortable monopoly position. (10)

2. The increase in costs resulting from environmental measures in the rich countries will again mean a serious deterioration in the exchange rate for the developing countries. Another way of expressing this is that the relative value of the raw materials com-

ponent, supplied by developing countries, in products of the highly industrialized countries, decreases compared to the necessary input of research and technology provided by the rich countries.

3. This increase in costs can be an extra reason or stimulus for the highly industrialized countries to protect their markets, even more than before, against competitive products from underdeveloped countries, which are, environmentally, still much better off in a number of respects, and will be wanting to take less stringent and costly measures. The Founex report deals with this matter in detail. (11) It acknowledges that there is a very real possibility of 'neo-protectionism' on the part of the rich countries, especially regarding agriculture and chemicals.

4. As the Founex report rightly remarks, concern for the environment in the highly industrialized countries can easily cause the already waning interest for development cooperation to decrease even more. Moreover, the danger exists that donor countries will impose their own stringent environmental standards, once they have been accepted within their own society, on developing countries and more especially will use them as conditions to the financing via development aid of certain projects in developing countries.

5. The technology of the highly industrialized countries, already highly unsuited to the needs of the majority of the population in the developing countries will, because of environmental measures, depart even further from these needs on a number of points. As long as a developing process on western lines, based on western technology is pursued in the Third World, increasingly larger financial costs will be involved; not to mention the 1.5 milliard dollars which according to an estimate by S. Patel were paid out in 1968 by developing countries as direct costs of the transfer of technology (patents, licences, know-how and technical aid). (12) Patel estimates the total annual costs, which the technological independence of the developing countries entails, at 6-12 milliard dollars.

6. The Founex report also mentions a number of points which can be of some profit to the developing countries. Synthetics will have to become more expensive and will then have more difficulty in competing with natural raw materials from developing countries (jute, sisal etc.).

7. Another aspect is described as follows:

'The developing countries can use the growing concern for social services in the developed world to escape from the tyranny of financial rates of return in traditional project appraisal, to seek broader international support for their social programmes in conformity with their own national priorities and to obtain a greater amount of local currency financing for these programmes and projects.'(13)

8. Removal of polluting industries to developing countries is regarded in the Founex report as a promising possibility if three requirements are fulfilled:
a. foreign investment occurs on conditions which are favourable for the developing country;
b. it results in a net transfer of means;
c. it satisfies the environmental standards which the receiving country wishes to impose in the light of its own development level and own cultural and social objectives.

These eight points require two comments. In the first place, it appears that for the time being, there are few quantitative indications about the extent of the effects. The Founex report mentions, for instance, vague estimates of 5-20% (!) regarding the increase of costs of non-polluting technology compared with the current technology. There is no doubt in our minds, however, that the cumulative effects for the developing countries will indeed be considerable if they are passed on in the customary way by the rich countries. In the second place, the Founex report makes some serious omissions. Gunnar Myrdal mentions three of them: not enough consideration is given to the population explosion, too little attention is paid to the physical climate in the underdeveloped countries as a direct and indirect factor obstructing development and the very unequal distribution of income and power in these countries is not even mentioned. Neither is any attention paid to the economic power which multinational enterprises are building up in our world, sometimes using soft and sometimes using hard methods. This power is soberly but emphatically described by Stephen Hymer. (14) Within the context of environmental problems, this power will only be strengthened further because the concern will fulfil a pronouncedly key role in the development and commercialization of the advanced technology which is generally considered necessary for environmental control. Japanese multinationals in particular have already begun to transfer polluting subsidiary enterprises to developing countries.

3. Effects of the Green Revolution

Publicity about the prolonged calamitous drought in the Sahel countries at the beginning of the seventies and the simultaneous failure of grain and rice harvests in a number of places in the world has once again brought the world food problem to the attention of the public. The present situation is alarming enough. In one of his latest books 'l'Utopie ou la Mort' the French agronomist, René Dumont quotes the Director General of the FAO, Boerma, who stated on 20th November, 1972, that the growth of agricultural production in the Third World was, in 1972 about 1% instead of the anticipated

4%. This growth was also 1% in 1971. Boerma adds, 'The failure of one year can be regarded as an exception but two failures, one after the other, can no longer be accidental'. A little further on, René Dumont presents a number of figures from the FAO: At the beginning of the Indicative World Plan for agriculture, it was anticipated that the percentage of undernourished people in the total world population would be reduced by 33% or 40% in 1972. In 1973, however, this percentage was seen to be almost the same as in 1962. This means that the number of undernourished people increases at the same rate as the world population and is estimated by the FAO to be between 300 and 500 million. Dumont considers this to be an optimistic estimate.

Putting aside the present situation for the moment, the prospects for the future have become much more sombre than they appeared to be in the late sixties during the 'break-through' of the Green Revolution. This can be attributed to a number of factors. We know, for instance, that the population explosion will in all probability lead to a total world population of 6-7 milliard people by the year 2000. While the population growth in the prosperous areas of the world will presumably be practically nihil by that time, the population of the countries at present underdeveloped - which will then constitute approximately four-fifths of the world population - will very probably continue to increase for a considerable length of time. Gunnar Myrdal makes a vague prognosis that 'will be realized soon after the year 2000, 10 milliard people and eventually 15 milliard and more'. (15)

This explosive population growth is a particularly frightening prospect for those parts of the world (South and South East Asia), where the problem of undernourishment has already assumed gigantic proportions. In a detailed study carried out in 1971, Dandekar and Rath reached the conclusion that with regard to their income levels 40% of the population of India live beneath the official poverty limit, fixed by the government. Below this limit, undernourishment because of lack of purchase power, begins. (16)

To what extent does the Green Revolution offer hope in this situation? By the Green Revolution we mean here the use of newly cultivated grain and rice varieties, that, subject to good irrigation, disease and insect control and especially considerable use of artificial fertilizers, enables a tremendous increase in the yield per hectare. The Green Revolution has spread fairly rapidly in a number of areas in the Third World. This is shown by the Tables 1 and 2. The Green Revolution has led to an increase of the already wide divergences in average welfare between individual areas in various countries: because good irrigation is at this stage an absolute necessity it is not directly possible to introduce the new varieties in dry or periodically flooded areas. In India, application is concentrated in the states in the north and north west, such as the Punjab. In Turkey, application is restricted to the low coastal land. In former East Pakistan, a delta area, practically none of

Table 1. Rice

	Percentage agricultural area sown with HYV* (1970-71)	Yield (100 kg. per hectare)		
		1948-52	1961-65	1969-70
Bangladesh	3.3			
Burma	4.0	14..6	16.4	17..0
Sri Lanka	4.5	14.2	19.1	24.5
India	14.7	11.1	14.8	16.6
Indonesia	11.3	16.1	18.1	20.0
South Korea	40.0	36.2	40.9	45.7
Laos	6.1	7.4	8.4	9.0
West Malaysia	24.5	19.3	25.0	25.5
Nepal	5.7	19.4	19.5	19.5
Pakistan	41.7			
The Philippines	49.8	11.8	12.6	17.3
Thailand	2.1	13.1	15.9	18.5
Suriname	7.0 (1968-69)	29.4	28.8	33.3
Taiwan	73.8	23.2	36.7	39.3
South Vietnam	19.8	13.6	20.4	21.8

* (High Yielding Varieties): the new seed varieties which make the
Green Revolution possible.
Source: Food and the New Agricultural Technology, UNRISD report
no. 72-9.

the attempts was successful, while in West Pakistan, the Green
Revolution has been very successful from the point of view of increasing agricultural production. As soon as all the irrigated areas
have been reached by the Green Revolution, further expansion
stagnates. With regard to India, the FAO, in its 1972 report,
called the stagnation alarming. (17)
Even more important is the intensification of class distinctions as
a result of the Green Revolution. Harry Cleaver jr. makes the
following comment at the end of his well-documented article on
the contrasts of the Green Revolution in Monthly Review, June 1972:

'The problem of hunger in the capitalist world has seldom been
one of absolute food shortage, especially when the production capacity of the developed countries is taken into account. It is a
problem of unequal distribution, caused by a system which feeds
those who have money and which, except when forced to behave
differently, lets the others look after themselves. '(18)

It is beyond the scope of an article on environmental problems to go
into the pauperization and unemployment, which often accompany
the Green Revolution. The farmers who have much and good (irrigated) land at their disposal, make large profits; in a number of

Table 2. Wheat

	Percentage agricultural area sown with HYV* (1970-71)	Yield (100 kg. per hectare)		
		1948-52	1961-65	1969-70
Afghanistan	7. 8	8. 5	9. 5	11. 4
Algeria	4. 7	6. 2	6. 4	5. 3
Bangladesh	7. 7			
India	32. 9	6. 6	8. 4	11. 9
Iran	3. 1	9. 0	8. 0	8. 6
Iraq	6. 2	4. 8	5. 3	5. 4
The Lebanon	5. 7	7. 0	9. 4	7. 6
Morocco	4. 0	6. 1	8. 5	8. 2
Nepal	49. 1	9. 1	10. 9	12. 2
Pakistan	48. 7	8. 7	8. 3	11. 3
Syria	10. 1	7. 7	7. 8	6. 5
Tunisia	14. 0	4. 9	4. 5	4. 9
Turkey	5. 8	10. 0	10. 8	12. 0
Mexico	90. 0 (1970)	8. 0	20. 2	29. 0

* HYV (High Yielding Varieties): the new seed varieties which make the Green Revolution possible.
Source: Food and the New Agricultural Technology, UNRISD report no. 72-9.

cases this leads to further expansion of their property and labour-replacing mechanization at the expense of small farmers and land labourers, who in general do not, or hardly profit from the Green Revolution.
In the abovementioned article, Harry Cleaver points out that perhaps the most devastating consequences, which a Green Revolution carried out on a large scale could have, are the consequences for the ecosystem. (19)
Although we can, to an extent, manipulate nature, as the producer of our food, it is clear that there is a limit somewhere. That limit is indicated either by the lack of one of the natural elements necessary for the growth of the food crops: water or (fertile) soil, or because insecticides and other substances, used by modern agriculture, are making the environment unfit to live in. According to Lester Brown:

'Where man's supply of food is concerned, the question is no longer whether we can produce enough food but, rather, what are the environmental consequences of doing so. As we confront the latter question, there is growing doubt as to whether the earth's agricultural ecosystem can both sustain an end-of-century population of 6. 5 billion and accommodate the universal desire on the part of the world's hungry for a much better diet. '(20)

Lester Brown estimates the amount of food required annually at the end of this century at about three times the present production because of the increase of population and effective demand. (He should also have included here food-gifts for the population groups with no purchasing power.) What are, roughly, the ecological obstacles to this growth?

1. If it is to be a growth in the breadth, i.e. in a further reclamation of marginal land, entailing the removal of the original carpet of undergrowth, the problem of erosion of the thin layer of humus through wind and water soon arises. According to the agronomist René Dumont, this has already reached very serious proportions in tropical areas and he presents the following estimates: (21) from 1882-1952, 15% of the cultivated land in the developing countries became unsuited for further exploitation. In 1952, it was estimated that 39.4% had lost at least half of its layer of humus, compared to 10% in 1882. It was estimated that the percentage of good agricultural land had decreased during these 70 years from 85% to 41%. Dumont does say, however, that these estimates only give an i n d i c a t i o n of the extent of the problem. Like many others, he warns against underestimation. A good soil structure, the product of millions of years of natural balance and life and death cycles, can be irreparably destroyed within a few years. According to Dumont, even in the USA, where enormous investments have been made in programmes aimed at protecting the fertility of the country, 10-11 million hectares have been spoiled by erosion, to some degree.
Barbara Ward (22) also emphasizes the fact that the ecological risks of hasty reclamation and cultivation are greater in the tropics than in the moderate zone because of three factors: the vulnerability of the soil, the nature of the rainfall and the high temperatures. In her opinion, this means that the Green Revolution must be accompanied by a completely new approach, including agricultural research and careful experimentation. Activities in China have shown the possibilities arising from the mobilization of the masses for new reclamations, soil improvement, combating erosion but also for drainage and dyke-building and the construction of irrigation facilities. Land and human labour are eminently the production factors which the developing countries will have to work with. In order to make the land more productive and to protect it, labour-intensive public works on a large scale are the best means. (23)

2. As we have mentioned above, there are two limits to any intensification of the cultivation of the present area: lack of water and damage to the environment by excessive use of insecticides. In 1967, a total of 1400 milliard m^3 (fresh) water was used for irrigation in the world, i.e. 70% of all water consumed. The FAO estimates that in the year 2000, the consumption of water by industry and direct human consumption will have increased so much that only 51% of all consumable water will be available for irrigation,

i.e. about 2800 milliard m^3. (24) Lester Brown is of the opinion that shortage of water could eventually induce man to take unconventional and, for the earthly environment, very risky steps, such as extracting the salt from sea water by atomic energy and inducing changes in the earthly climate.

The consequences which can arise from an increasing intervention in the earthly environment in order to satisfy an increasing need for food can be illustrated somewhat dramatically by the case of DDT. DDT is one of the persistent and strong agricultural toxins which, contrary to a substance such as parathion, can accumulate in the tissue of living organisms. Similarly to other chloridated hydrocarbons, DDT resembles the poisonous heavy metals mercury, arsenic and lead in this respect. As early as 1950, it was known that once discharged into the environment, these metals tend to accumulate in the biological food chain and ultimately reach food destined for human consumption. An excessive use of DDT was seen to have a similar effect. According to Lester Brown, there is more DDT in the breast milk of nursing mothers than is allowed by the Food and Drug Administration. (25)

In a recent investigation, three American scientists attempted to give an insight into the amounts of DDT which have been produced and the proportion of DDT which, at the end of the sixties, had accumulated in land, water and living organisms on earth, via all kinds of cycles. They reached the conclusion that living organisms contain considerably less DDT than would be expected on grounds of the amounts produced and circulating. The reason for this is unknown. Their conclusion is as follows:

'The analysis suggests that mere good fortune has protected man and the rest of the biota from much higher concentrations, thus emphasizing the need to determine the details of the movement of DDT residues and other toxins through the biosphere and to move swiftly to bring world use of such toxins under rational control based on firm knowledge of local and worldwide cycles and hazards. '(26)

In the meantime, propagandists of the Green Revolution continue to consider the use of DDT necessary in order to cope with an impending food crisis. Barbara Ward, however, advocates a much more careful use of insecticides and a gradual abolition of DDT. An additional reason for this is that DDT has a fatal effect on all insects as well as on disease-producing bacteria and viruses. In this way, the natural enemies of these disease carriers are often destroyed. By the time the disease carriers have become resistant to DDT, they can, in the absence of their natural enemies, develop freely. Harry Cleaver attributes the massive and irresponsible use of these kinds of 'all purpose' insecticides to the production and marketing policy of the large chemical companies in particular. The enlargement of the market for remedies such as DDT, which

have an all-destroying effect (instead of a specific effect on one or
several disease-carriers or insects, as urged by Barbara Ward)
adds directly to the net profit of these firms. In order to provide the necessary incentive for research aimed at finding alternatives for DDT and other persistent and strong agricultural toxins,
Barbara Ward urges that a deadline be fixed for the gradual prohibition of these substances.
The FAO has estimated the minimum cost of having access to sufficient improved seed varieties, artificial fertilizers and irrigation
water for the Green Revolution at roughly 50 milliard dollars' worth
of cumulative investments in 1985. Barbara Ward estimates the
additional amount required for complementary investments in physical infrastructure, technical-scientific research, cooperations,
transport and agricultural guidance to be double this sum. Where is
this financing to come from?

The question whether our earthly ecosystem could feed 7 milliard
people is therefore too theoretical. The question should be whether
we can emerge from the present situation, in which hundreds of
millions of people are undernourished into a situation of balance
between population and food supply, so that the number of undernourished people in the world not only stops increasing (which is
what it does now), but decreases. This means that we not only have
to keep up with the population growth but have to make up much
leeway in food supply activities. Heilbronner is justified in saying: (27)
'We do not have to wait for gigantic inevitable famine: it has already
come'. He is not merely referring to famines and the continual
quantitative lack of food, to which hundreds of millions of people are
exposed day in day out, but also the insufficiently adjusted diet and
especially the protein deficiency in the diet of young children. Once
again, we must point out that this problem, i.e. the quality of the
diet is also caused by social inequality, although not exclusively.
Underdeveloped countries export large quantities of excellent prote-
in-rich food to rich countries in order to enable overfeeding there
and sometimes to provide the raw materials for pet food. For
instance, one third of all fish caught in Peru is processed into fish
meal, practically all of which is exported to the rich countries and
is earmarked for cattle feed.
Lester Brown has calculated that the average consumption of grain
per inhabitant in the developing countries is approximately 180 kg.
per year. Of this, 75 kg. is consumed directly but the rest indirectly,
mainly as meat, milk and eggs. (28) It takes 7 calories of vegetable
food to obtain 1 calorie of animal food. The rapid rise in meat consumption in the prosperous countries means therefore that an increasing part of world agriculture is aimed at the production of
cattle feed. By American standards, the total world agricultural
production could only feed 1 milliard people. (In the meantime,
there are still people in the USA who die from malnutrition.)
The problem of how to feed the Third World must, in the first place
be solved by the Third World itself, by means of an intensive and

extensive expansion of agriculture. The technical knowhow necessary for this must be developed further. The social structure found in many countries obstructs the application of these techniques. Because of the very unequal ownership ratios, only a small proportion of farmers profit by the new developments. In addition, the ecological risks and obstacles are becoming increasingly important. Only a thorough revision of the present social structure can make more people amenable to an increase in agricultural production and also enable them to profit from it, as well as reduce the ecological risks involved.

4. International environmental control: the ocean

An important decision will soon have to be made within the framework of the United Nations, since it must be decided how the ocean and the ocean bed should be controlled in the future. What are the elements of this problem? Some of the ideas of Prof. Logue, expressed in detail in 'World Federalist' (29) are summarized below:

a. At present, the ocean is used as the sole rubbish dump of all mankind. Unlike the rivers, the ocean cannot dispose of the matter it absorbs. Insecticides, lead, arsenic, waste, oil and radio activity accumulate and constitute an increasing danger to the life that is present in the ocean, but also to human life on earth, insofar as it is dependent on the sea, for food.

b. Maritime armament (atomic submarines equipped with rockets and espionage systems) is the heart of the military apparatus of the super powers.

c. The riches of the ocean, especially the oil and minerals from the sea bed, are very extensive and could constitute an invaluable source of aid for the developing countries and an independent source of finance for the United Nations.

d. The international rules of law for the ocean are obsolete. A dramatic race is in process between new increasingly larger claims which national states lay on the sea bed and its wealth and the attempts by the United Nations to place a considerable part of the sea bed under common control. (In 1958, the Geneva Convention on International Maritime Law, gave the coastal states sovereignty to a depth of 200 metres but the treaty included a clause that the coastal states were to be allowed to claim an extra part of the sea bed, if it became 'exploitable'. As far as we know, most of the wealth is not situated in the deep sea bed, but in the higher parts of the ocean bed, near the coast.

e. It follows from all this that institutions will and must come which are given international authority in these matters. Only the character of these international bodies has yet to be determined.

f. Finally: all these aspects are related to the fantastic progress that has been made in the field of 'ocean technology'. At this moment, one fifth of the oil in the world is extracted from the bottom of the sea. In 1980, this may well be one third.

In 1974, a large and important Conference of the United Nations was held on Maritime Law. The most important points settled at this conference concerned the demarcation of the boundary of the territorial area and the nature of the international controlling body. The basis for this conference was the resolution accepted by the General Assembly of the United Nations in 1970, in which the sea bottom was declared to be 'common heritage of mankind' and outside the bounds of national jurisdiction. The clause in the abovementioned Geneva Convention leads to an increasingly extensive appropriation of valuable deposits in the sea bed by coastal states which possess sufficient technological capacity to exploit them. There is a search for oil at depths of 900 metres, although in 1973 the exploitation was still limited to depths less than 200 metres. It is estimated that half of the possible oil reserves in the world are to be found in the sea bed up to depths of 2,500 metres. The speed of technological development is such that the maximum depth at which oil and gas can be commercially exploited increases by almost 100 metres each year. (30)

Consequently, those countries in which modern technology, financial means and the powers of organization are concentrated (which therefore excludes the developing countries), gradually obtain more control over increasingly larger mineral reserves.

However, the sea bed is not the only potential source of conflict. Countries with a large fishing industry are extremely concerned about pollution, about exhaustion of the fish supplies and about foreign fishing fleets in their own waters. On the other hand they are only too eager to keep on fishing near someone else's coast. Countries with atomic power are afraid that extension of the territorial waters will impede the mobility, and especially the transit through certain straits, of their atomic submarines.

Finally, the ocean is more than a source of material wealth; it is also used as garbage dump. An international group of marine biologists, who met in 1971 at the Conference Pacem in Maribus, were unanimous in the conclusion that life in the sea was being seriously endangered by increasing pollution. Barbara Ward illustrates the situation by describing what has happened with Lake Erie in the USA. The pollution in this lake has now reached a level which is so serious that it would have been considered impossible some decades ago. It would take 10 times the length of Lake Erie to span the Atlantic Ocean. The ocean is of course much deeper but as Mulckhuyse has observed, the pollution which enters the sea from the rivers and via the atmosphere is not spread out evenly over the whole ocean, but remains concentrated in the uppermost ocean layers (100-200 metres). Moreover, the ocean, contrary to Lake Erie, has no outlet and is not just polluted by a number of large cities but by thousands of rivers and lakes, which discharge the waste and pollution of the whole world. This includes very poisonous substances such as lead compounds, arsenic, mercury compounds and DDT.

The heart of the problem is that without knowing exactly what the effect of the large scale discharge of waste matter in the marine environment will be, we still continue producing and discharging this matter, much of which c a n be fatal to the life in the sea and thereby indirectly to human life on land. This ignorance regarding potential consequences was revealed in a particularly dramatic way in the case of mercury. (31) It had long been thought that mercury, being indissoluble in water, would cause no serious danger, i. e. by poisoning the food chains in the sea. In 1953, however, the population around the bay of Minamata in Japan appeared to be suffering from a serious neurological disorder. The patients lost control over their movements, could no longer speak, or became paralyzed. In some cases, insanity even appeared. In the ensuing years, at least 116 people were afflicted. These included 19 children who were born deformed. 43 patients died. When this sickness appeared again in 1956, elsewhere in Japan, and 30 people were smitten, 5 of whom died, it was discovered that the cause was to be found in the consumption of fish. This fish had been caught in water that was polluted by mercury. How did this mercury become dissolved? Certain micro-organisms found in sludge and rotting material appeared to be able to convert mercury into the compound methylmercury which dissolves in water, is extremely poisonous and is easily absorbed and concentrated by living organisms. In October 1973, in the Japanese city Kumamoto, 44 people died through mercurial poisoning. The mercury came from waste discharged into the sea. The dangers of mercury are now beyond doubt, although much too little action is taken against it. The dangerous aspects of a large number of other substances, however, which are found in our waste or which fall into the sea via the atmosphere, are not even known yet. What we do know, however, is so alarming, that immediate action is imperative. Mulckhuyse is justified in concluding: (32)

'Although the systematic data known as yet about the pollution of the ocean are few, we can already ascertain that the discharge of certain waste matter and the production and consumption of certain matter will have to be severely restricted or prohibited in order to prevent catastrophical poisoning symptoms from appearing in the communities of life on earth, which also includes man. International cooperation is essential here because various problems fall outside the jurisdiction of the individual countries. '

5. Final comments

The image we have evoked by our foregoing remarks is not particularly cheerful ... This is mainly because the international cooperation between rich and poor countries has reached an impasse if there ever has even been any real international cooperation at all between the two groups of countries. As we have indicated above, the Third World will feel a considerable repercussion from environmental measures which the rich countries decide to take on their own. If the Green Revolution is really to solve the food problem in the Third World, the attitude of the rich countries will need to undergo a profound change. They will, for instance, have to stop exorbitant protection of their own agriculture because only then can the world markets for agricultural products be regulated so that they constitute a stable and favourable climate for development of agriculture in the Third World, apart from the planning of emergency supplies and the provision of food for distressed population groups. Recent diplomatic tangles regarding the control of the ocean have shown finally that many developing countries which happen to be coastal states, are supporters of a very large territorial area (e. g. up to 200 miles from the coast) which would mean that the most important known riches from the ocean bed, i. e. the oil and gas reserves on the continental shelf, would no longer fall under the 'common heritage of mankind'.

Evidently, these developing countries do not believe that a supranational ocean regime which would have more collective riches under its control, will bring much benefit to themselves. World society exhibits the alarming pattern of sovereign states competing with each other, with a number of states rising head and shoulders above the rest in power and prosperity and exploiting the others economically. The structure of international economic (and political) relations is in fact determined mainly by the interests of the rich countries. It is their balance of payments problems and inflation which cause the international monetary crises, and their production pattern dominates the world economy to a considerable degree. In particular, their populations pollute the sea, either through the discharge of industrial waste and household rubbish or by oil transports and oil drillings, not to mention the military-strategic division of the world into spheres of influence by the rich countries. If international initiatives are being considered to cope with the energy crisis, to develop commercially the recycling of scarce raw materials or to limit and control the discharge of poisonous matter into the sea, then these initiatives are looked for too often in the field of improved East-West relations and the OECD, the NATO or the EEC. The Third World, as the rest of the world is called - for the sake of convenience - often remains a spectator. The reality of the material unity of the earth does, however, require the introduction of supra-national decision-making bodies.

Whoever attempts to review human existence on earth in its entirety, and tries to understand the nature of our situation cannot avoid the feeling which René Dumont describes in his book 'l'Utopie ou la Mort':'J'ai été véritablement saisi à la gorge par les perspectives ainsi évoquées'. (33) Dumont considers revolutions in the poor countries and ecological catastrophes in the rich countries (may they be kept within bounds) to be inevitable. 'Les riches et les puissants, et même les semi-privilégiés que nous sommes, ne réaliseront le danger de l'évolution actuelle qu'au moment où ils en suffriront personnellement et gravement.'(34) How true is this? It would mean that the population in rich countries would only be stirred up by environmental calamities and not by ignoble poverty and hunger in the Third World.

At any rate, it is of the utmost importance that as many people as possible become conscious of this as soon as possible. 'Le seul espoir réside alors dans une prise de conscience bien plus rapide, par le plus grand nombre, de l'extrême gravité de la situation.'(35) The world situation as described above, could be compared with a passenger ship on the high seas. There are two different groups of people on board - a smaller group, occupying the first class apartments fore, and a large group accommodated at the stern. The ship has sprung a leak at the back and is filling with water. The passengers at the stern have no pumps at their disposal. The only pumps on the ship are in the first class apartments and are all used to pump fresh water out of the sea for the showers and saunas of the guests.

There is no commander on board. There is, however, a united ship's council, in which representatives of both groups of passengers consult together without obligation. The matter of the pumps had been brought up but because there were many first class passengers who considered that, compared to others, they already had too little opportunity to have a shower, the matter had been set aside, despite the objections of the representatives from the stern....

Notes and List of references

1. Aurelio Peccei and Manfred Siebker, 'Point and Counterpoint: a Summary of the Debate over The Limits to Growth', in: IDOC International, North American Edition, no. 52, April 1973.
2. Development and Environment, Report submitted by a Panel of Experts, June 1971, 1.4. (Founex report).
3. Barbara Ward and René Dubos, Only One Earth, 1972, p. 295.
4. Barbara Ward writes in The Economist (27th May, 1972): 'In concrete terms, the next American baby will make 500 times more claims on the earth's resources than any child born in India or Chad or Mongolia'.
5. Two Dutch books on applied ecology are: Biosfeer en mens, Centrum voor Landbouwpublikaties en Landbouwdokumentatie, Wageningen, 1970; and Het verstoorde evenwicht, publ. Oosthoek, 1970.
6. Cf. also the well-known popular work on this matter by Pierre Teilhard de Chardin, Le phénomène humain, Paris, 1955.
7. G. Picht, Die Demontage der Natur - ökologische Krise und industrielle Planung, in: Evangelische Kommentare, April 1972.
8. Stanford Biology Study Group, A Legacy of Our Presence, The Destruction of Indochina, 1970.

This publication presents an alarming survey of the two main environmental destruction programmes used by the USA during the latter years of the Vietnam war. The three-fold aim of this campaign, a crime against environment and man was, according to the American army, to starve out the civilian population and soldiers who remained in the regions controlled by the Viet Cong, to prevent ambushes along heavily forested roads and rivers and to expose the headquarters of the Revolutionary Army and its supply routes.

9. Barbara Ward, op. cit., p. 285. Her definition of 'techno-sphere' is:'The constructed world order of technological innovation, investment flows and commercial exchanges'.
10. Gunnar Myrdal points out this possibility in his article 'Economics of an improved environment', in: International Technical Cooperation Centre Review, vol. 2, no. 2 (6) April 1973. Whether or not this effect appears depends of course on the allied substitution-elasticity.
11. Founex report, op. cit., Chapter 4, passim.
12. Surendra J. Patel, The cost of the technological dependence, in: Ceres, March-April 1973.
13. Patel, op. cit., 4.13.
14. Stephen Hymer, The Multinational Corporation and the Law of uneven Development. Center Paper, no. 181, Yale University, 1972.
15. Gunnar Myrdal, op. cit., p. 29. Myrdal's estimates are very vague. They do, however, fit in with the projections which Tomas Frejka gives in his book The Future of Population Growth, 1973.
16. V. M. Dandekar and N. Rath, 'Poverty in India', in: Economic and Political Weekly, vol. VI, no. 1/2, Jan. 1971.
17. See: R. Dumont, l'Utopie ou la Mort, p. 26.
18. A translation of Harry Cleaver's article, together with some other critical articles on the Green Revolution, can be found in Nesbic-bulletin, vol. 7, no. 8, Sept. 1972, 'De Groene Revolutie: katalysator van de onderontwikkeling'.
19. Harry Cleaver has thus joined an already sizeable company, which includes Mansholt and Dumont. With Cleaver however, the accent is clearly on the criticism of the capitalist organizational structure of the Green Revolution. In his opinion, this causes the ecological risks to be much greater than strictly necessary, technically speaking. See article in Nesbic-bulletin, referred to in no. 18.
20. Lester Brown, The Environmental Consequences of Man's Quest for Food, in: Peter Albertson and Margery Barnett (eds.), Managing the Planet, 1972, p. 46.
21. R. Dumont, l'Utopie ou la Mort, p. 30.
22. Barbara Ward and René Dubos, Only One Earth, p. 224.
23. It must be noted here that the organization of these kinds of public works is very difficult. It appears that even in China, serious mistakes were made in the years 1958-1960, and it is

only because of the extent of the work that was indeed successful, that the ultimate balance of the results during these
years probably tends to be positive. See, e. g. E. L. Wheel-
wright and Bruce McFarlane, The Chinese Road to Socialism,
1970.

24. Data derived from R. Dumont, op. cit. , pp. 33-34.
25. Data derived from Lester Brown, op. cit. See also, Robert
    Heilbronner, 'Ecological Armageddon', in: Johnson and
    Hardesty (eds.), Economic Growth versus the Environment,
    1971.
26. Science, 10 Dec. 1971.
27. Heilbronner, op. cit. (note 25).
28. Lester Brown, op. cit. , p. 43.
29. J. J. Logue, 'What is the ocean problem?', in: World Federalist,
    World edition, March/April 1972.
30. The Economist, 1 Sept. 1973.
31. Data on the mercury poisoning affair in Japan are derived from
    Barbara Ward and René Dubos, op. cit. ; J. J. Mulckhuyse,
    'Moeten wij de oceaan degraderen tot vuilnisbelt?', in: Inter-
    mediair, vol. 7, no. 39; Michael Harwood, 'Stervende Ocea-
    nen', in: Volkskrant, 26-10-1971 and De Tijd, 16-10-1973.
32. J. J. Mulckhuyse, loc. cit.
33. R. Dumont, op. cit. , p. 10.
34. R. Dumont, op. cit. , p. 148.
35. R. Dumont, ibid.

Contents Vol. 2

32, 60